*This book is a must read for anyone in management.
Enda Larkin does an excellent job of simplifying the
complexities of management through story-telling.
Journeys will engage and entertain you from the start
whilst providing you with many practical tools and tips.
It is a real gem.*
Deirdre Clohessy, HR Manager, Toyota Ireland

*Enda Larkin's book on the art of management should be
required reading for all managers. Not only is his method
of conveying key messages much more interesting
(stories!) than the average management book, he avoids
the idea that there's a one-size-fits-all approach to
management. Rather, he encourages readers to find their
own lessons in the stories. An entertaining and thought-
provoking read.*
**Siobhan Cleary, Director: Strategy and Public Policy,
Johannesburg Stock Exchange**

*Leadership is a great and never-ending learning journey.
Enda´s book offers actions and insights from a human,
fun and provocative management experience. This is not
only a book about making people happier at work but
about the way we interact with people in our lives.*
**Marcelo Furtado, Executive Director, Greenpeace
Brazil**

This book provides a powerful insight into management whether you are a rookie or a veteran in the business world. The anecdotal format allows for complex insights to be communicated in simple bite size chunks. A must-read, especially for all aspiring business leaders.
Bernard Farrell, Managing Director - CIS Division, Quinn Manufacturing Group

Essential reading that, through the medium of storytelling, will assist managers to face the challenge of successfully leading and inspiring teams in today's demanding business environment.
Gerard Denneny, Hotel Manager, Jumeirah Essex House, New York

JOURNEYS

Short Stories and Tall Tales for Managers

Enda Larkin

Published by OAK TREE PRESS, 19 Rutland Street, Cork, Ireland
www.oaktreepress.com

© 2012 Enda Larkin

A catalogue record of this book is available from the British Library.

ISBN 978 1 78119 032 6 (Paperback)
ISBN 978 1 78119 033 3 (ePub)
ISBN 978 1 78119 034 0 (Kindle)

An old man sat studying just outside of the gates of an ancient city. A traveler approached him saying, "Old man, tell me what are the people like in this city?"

The old man looked up from his reading and said, "First tell me what the people were like in your home city?"

"The people in my home city were a miserable lot, greedy and mean-spirited. They are why I left to wander the cruel world. I have vowed never to return to that horrible place."

The old man sadly looked up and said, "Sir, I am afraid you will find the people in this city to be much the same."

The traveler shook his head in disgust and passed by the city gates.

A few minutes later another traveler approached and bowing to the old man said, "Venerable one, may I ask you to tell me of the people in this beautiful place?"

Again the old man asked, "First tell me what the people were like in your home city?"

The young man smiled and said, "It is a place much blessed, the people are kind and generous, I look forward to the time when my travels carry me back home so I can tell them of all the wonders I have seen."

The old man smiled and said, "Sir, I am happy to tell you that you will find the people in this city to be much the same. Welcome."

Attributed to Khalil Gibran, Lebanese American artist, poet, and writer

CONTENTS

ACKNOWLEDGEMENTS

Thanks to Martina, without whose inspiration and support this book would not have happened.

Thanks also to Brian O'Kane at Oak Tree Press for all his help in publishing this book.

INTRODUCTION

"There are known knowns. These are things we know that we know. There are known unknowns. That is to say, there are things that we know we don't know. But there are also unknown unknowns. There are things we don't know we don't know."

Fair enough, if you say so, Mr. Rumsfeld.

What I think the former US Defense Secretary was getting at, as he offered this memorable 'clarification' to reporters on one occasion during the Iraq War, was that we do not have all the answers in any given situation. Life is full of uncertainties and imponderables. So too is the world of work; there is plenty that we still do not fully understand about management, particularly when it relates to intangibles such as human nature and behavior. Having said that, there are lots of known knowns too when it comes to organizational life.

And three of them in particular have informed this book.

The first of those known knowns is that over-complicating matters is rarely a good idea, regardless of the context involved. As a general rule in most fields of human endeavor, the majority of people like to keep things as straightforward as possible; after all the KISS principle (keep it simple, stupid) did not become a popular mantra for nothing.

Yet to look at the subject of management, you would imagine that no one involved had ever heard of that principle, or so you might assume when you consider how the hype and complexity surrounding the topic have spiraled out of control in recent years. Take a quick browse through the business section of any bookstore (physical or online) and see just how many ways there are to say essentially the same thing. When it comes to management we sped past overkill quite some time ago and the topic is now swamped in competing concepts, models and an unbelievable amount of jargon.

It can be truly mind-boggling at times.

Managing and leading (those distinctions will be addressed later in this book) undeniably are big challenges and nobody in their right mind would argue otherwise. But outside of the undoubtedly essential business models and systems, the route map for success is to be found – where it has always been – firmly embedded within the sphere of human relations. At the heart of being a great manager lie some fundamental, commonsense principles that guide all human interactions and business activities. These remain the same no matter how much they might be dolled up at times.

Simplicity is best and that core principle has guided the development of this book – but do not confuse lack of glitter with lack of substance.

A second known known that has influenced the approach taken in this book is the growing body of research, and indeed anecdotal evidence, indicating that our reading habits are changing quite significantly, particularly in relation to the business genre. Certainly there is a shift from print to electronic formats but in general a variety of studies show that reading rates, especially for younger people, are declining. That is not to say that reading is dying out – far from it – but the 'cover-to-cover' approach is becoming less prevalent today for business subjects than it once was. People favor more targeted reading, especially online, that responds to their specific or immediate needs.

Add to this the additional research that shows our attention spans are shortening. By how much they are falling is open to debate, but a number of studies support the idea that we are all less able to focus on a particular topic now than we were in the past. One study carried out by researchers in Britain found that an average person's attention span today is about five minutes compared to 12 minutes a decade ago.

Whatever the precise nature of the ongoing changes to our reading habits and attention spans, there are clearly significant challenges presented in terms of communicating important management messages. In response this book uses a still largely overlooked medium in business life – storytelling – to explore common management themes.

Learning through storytelling is hardly a foreign concept for any of us; as children, it played a major role in helping us to know what we now know. There is no reason, therefore, why well-written and meaningful stories cannot support learning in adulthood, and especially for a scenario-based topic like management.

The third known known that has informed this book, particularly its title, is the fact that improving as a manager requires a career-long effort: it is a journey of sorts. And on that journey too often experience and progression through the management ranks can cloud our view of self, creating a false sense of security that future success simply requires more of the same; a belief that what has worked so far will work again into the future.

Perhaps in an imaginary world where time stood still this might be true, but managers today must manage in an ever-changing environment. In particular, employees expect a lot more from their leaders, so a failure to respond to those changes essentially means falling behind. What is more, does anyone truly believe that 'more of the same' will suffice, given what has happened to the world of work in recent years?

Management capacity, particularly in terms of the soft skills required, therefore must be constantly strengthened. This book can help to support that developmental journey by allowing the reader to learn from realistic and practical scenarios. The stories presented span many life-cycle challenges facing managers, from the basic concepts applicable at the early career stage, to the increasingly complex problems, such as how to manage organizational change, that confront more experienced managers.

So the choice of content, format and title for this book has been driven by the fact that raising management performance requires continuous focus and effort over the long-term as well as the need to keep things simple and to make the content as appealing as possible.

As a result *Journeys* is a book of stories, real-world and work-related perhaps, but stories nonetheless. They are tales for managers: always about leadership and often about life. Each of the 15 stories ahead is based on actual occurrences and explores a different aspect of management. Many are linked by common themes and characters but all promote the view that our potential for success – in business and beyond – is directly influenced by the interplay between our attitudes, attributes and actions. To excel in any management role we constantly must reflect upon who we are, how we think and what we do.

First and foremost I genuinely hope that you enjoy reading these stories because I have written them with that aim in mind. In the process I am confident that you will gain some valuable insights about yourself to guide your future development.

These tales, shaped as they are by current management theory, my own extensive experience and by the many real-world leadership lessons I have learned from other people and situations, will take you on a stimulating journey through management life covering a spectrum of topics, from the attributes and skills required to lead effectively to the pitfalls associated with handling conflict. As the themes and characters unfold they will serve as a vehicle to help you to think about your own performance.

There are many lessons to be found woven between the lines of the stories that follow but the specific lessons identified will vary from reader to reader, for there is no attempt here to teach, or indeed to preach. Rather the intention is that each story should be read, enjoyed and then reflected upon. And from those reflections you may pinpoint aspects of who you are, or how you think, that could be holding you back. You also might discover elements of what you do that could benefit from improvement. The important point to note is that it will be you who decides which insights are of most value to you: the stories guide but do not dictate.

Y
ou might be fairly early in your management career at this point or maybe you are still just thinking about making that first step into a leadership role. Alternatively you could be an old hand at the management game, someone who has 'been there and done that' as they say. Whatever your existing title or level on the ladder *Journeys* offers you a chance, in an enjoyable yet substantive way, to reflect on your current strengths and areas for improvement. And even though the themes contained within these stories are not entirely new, your focus should be less on novelty and more on whether you apply these core principles and practices of management for best effect each and every working day.

If you are just starting out on your management journey the tales can help you first to identify and then avoid some common pitfalls faced by all managers. For more experienced managers there are plenty of useful thought-provokers here too, once you do not let the old dog in you overlook any new tricks that could prove helpful.

For the busy reader the tales are mostly written so that they can be read independently, but for greatest impact, I strongly recommend that you read them sequentially as the content subtly builds from one to the next.

No matter how you decide to advance through the stories, as you do so, do not just self-assess your own performance as a manager; instead, also consider what your direct reports and superiors actually think of your abilities. Are you considered by those around you to be an effective manager? Is *that* a known known?

Enjoy the read.

Enda Larkin
Geneva
February 2012

A man who carries a cat by the tail learns something he can learn in no other way.

Mark Twain

WORDS OF WISDOM

"Hey, Boss, what would be the key management lesson you would leave us with after all these years?"

Dave, my then second-in-command, was always playing games of one sort or another so I swung around to eyeball him. As he sipped his beer I tried to figure out whether his question was for real, or if he was just hoping to get a bit of mileage out of me as he sometimes liked to try and do. He could be a bit of a button-pusher at times. If I let him, that is.

It was then that I felt the twinge of sadness.

What am I saying? A twinge …? It was far more serious than that. A helluva lot more. I remember it happened just after I swiveled my stool around, when each and every one of those familiar faces had flashed in front of me – as if in slow motion – and once I had fixed eyes on Dave. Bam! It crept up and whacked me. Out of nowhere I was blindsided by the force of emotion. *How am I going to leave it all behind after 40-odd years? What am I going to do now? Home to a big empty apartment every night? Chrissakes, I will have nothing to do every day.*

In that moment I was sucked down into a very strange place. I felt sad – no, it was more than that – panicked, yes, that's how it felt, like I was drowning or something. I had never experienced anything like it, not even in the heat of battle. I don't usually do maudlin, but it was definitely doing me at that point. *Soon, they'll be feeding me through a straw. Nah, I would never let it reach that point. But it could happen. After all, except for Mike, I am all alone. And he might turn on me again. Better talk to him about it. And I'm starting to forget stuff lately ... look, calm down, it's only little things. Everyone forgets their keys now and again. I've plenty of good years left ... oh, maybe the key thing is only the start? What if all my faculties go, just like happened to my father …?*

"Boss …? Boss …? Is everything okay?"

The voice brought me back. Well, not back exactly, but it did stop me sinking further. I needed a minute or two to pull myself together. I told Dave I was going to need another beer if he was hoping to get any free advice out of me that evening and as he turned to order, I excused myself and made a bee-line for the restroom.

Standing alone in that cubicle the passage of time weighed heavily upon me. I really hadn't felt the years speed by, but they had. Like a shot, they were gone. And there I was: career over, sitting in Molly's sharing a last few drinks with my team before heading to the Four Seasons for a formal retirement dinner to be held in my honor later that evening. I pulled myself together, well sort of, stepped out of the cubicle, scorned the face in the mirror, splashed and dried it, and headed back out.

"Here's the beer, Boss. Now quit stalling! Hit us with one last great insight."

Despite the pseudo-sarcasm, I knew then from the look on his face that Dave genuinely did want to hear what I had to say; or more accurately he wanted those in the bar who, from the following Monday would be calling him boss, to hear what I had to say. He needed my past style of management to continue into the future under his reign. Why? Because, for one, he knew it worked. Period. Plus he would also be under a lot of pressure to keep the performance bar where he found it – up high – so he couldn't afford to let things slide when I was gone.

And a few words from me might go some small way to helping ensure that didn't happen. He played the innocent sometimes did Dave, but he was far from it.

I could feel all eyes around the bar lock on me in anticipation, waiting for my response, but for once, I was lost for words. Yes, the old soldier – The Big Kahuna – was sort of struck dumb. I clearly hadn't managed to leave all the emotion behind me in the restroom and all I could say, at first, was, "Keep it simple, guys ..."

There was an awkward silence when I said it too, like someone had died or something. Well, in one sense, there had actually been a death of sorts. A special moment had passed. And I had managed to kill it.

"Jeez, after 40 years, is that the best you can come up with, Boss?" said Dave, urging me with his eyes to say more. "Keep what simple?"

I took a big slug of beer to drown the soppiness once and for all. Then I started.

"Management. What else, Dave? That's what you asked me about after all, or did I miss something? Keep management simple. And what I mean is, cut out all the crap that seems to have attached itself to the topic of late. Free yourselves from all the hype and don't be afraid to go back to basics. Do the simple stuff, do it right, do it always and you'll all make good managers – or those of you who want that path in life will do so."

My next chug of beer washed away any traces of self-pity. I was back on track. And getting into my stride.

"Unfortunately like everything we do nowadays in business, people are constantly out there looking for the next big thing – the magic pill that will somehow give them the edge – with the result that management has become so shrouded in complexity. Chrissakes, when did you need a PhD to figure it all out? When did it all become so difficult to understand? And, hey, that's not just me being an old fogey before any of you young upstarts start giving me a hard time."

There was a bit of back-and-forth between the gang when I said that as to who actually qualified for the fogey and upstart categories.

Ah, the banter was always full-on when we got together as a group like that. I had regularly encouraged outside activities for my teams – but not always those which involved alcohol, mind you – and I did so because, for me, everything ultimately boiled down to the quality of the team: the better the team, the better the results. Sure I needed to be on top of my game as the figurehead, and of course our systems mattered too, but nothing was achieved without those guys.

Over the years I put a helluva lot of effort into making sure that the bonds between my key people stretched beyond the basics that came from working in the same place or for the same company. We really did share a common purpose. It was the glue that bound us together. And I was greatly rewarded for all that effort because I had some fantastic teams in my time.

I always got a real buzz being around them too, especially the younger crowd. I loved their energy, the vibe they had together and their enthusiasm for life. With this last group in particular – a great mix of young and wiser heads – we had achieved more than most. Oh sure, I pushed them, real hard, but they were up for it. They knew, and more importantly believed in what we were collectively trying to achieve and they went after it with all they had. Of course at times they didn't pull any punches with each other but behind all the bravado and trash-talk, they actually did care about one another. If you carried your weight with that crowd they looked out for you. But you had to stand up for yourself too.

Yes, my way had always been to keep things competitive within the firm, that's what I wanted, what I made happen. People show their best side, I believe, when they have to stretch themselves every day, to fight their corner – either that or they fall by the wayside.

But I never let competitive become aggressive. No damn way. I made sure that everyone knew where the line was with me, and indeed with each other. No bullies or egos allowed. I stuck to that rule for my whole career. I always moved people like that along as quickly as they showed their true colors, no matter how talented they were, or more usually, how talented they thought they were. Nope, too much downside with what the Irish call *Me Féiners* like them: individuals who only care about themselves. And that's what bullies and egos essentially are for me, selfish children looking to get their own way. That said, I certainly wanted strong people around me, but being tough didn't mean being an asshole in my book.

Anyway I'm sidetracking now. Once I pulled myself together that evening there was no stopping me – plus, with everyone having had a fair few beers on board, the questions started to fly.

"Give us an example of how we can simplify the management stuff, Boss?" asked one of the newer kids, part of the previous year's MBA intake who was semi-hidden at the back of the group.

Of course before I could actually get to answer that question, I had to let the wave of cat-calling die down between the other MBAs in the team who were ragging on the poor guy as to why he hadn't learned the answer on his 'second-rate' course. "If it ain't Ivy League, then it's only Little League," someone shouted, followed by cries of "Go Bulldogs" or whatever the college team chants were for those who shared an *Alma Mater*.

They're a funny lot, those MBA kids, always looking to let people know what schools they went to ... they never seemed to get the point that qualifications didn't matter a damn to me, other than they proved someone wasn't the village idiot – no, I mostly took people onboard because of who they were, not what they thought they knew, or what their ties or blazers told me about their backgrounds.

Sure the people I hired needed to be talented, that's a no-brainer, but you can build someone's skills and knowledge if there is a degree of intelligence there and more importantly, they have the right personality. I found to my cost over the years that it's much harder to teach someone not to be a jerk.

When they calmed down I answered his question.

"Well, one thing that really annoys me is how all the hype around management these days has made us lose sight of what we are supposed to do as managers: all this authentic, transformational, revolutionary stuff – who dreamt up that load of mumbo-jumbo? My belief is that you should try to keep it simple and never forget what management is really about, or what managers are supposed to be and do."

At that point one of the geekier MBAs in the team actually proceeded to list some of the names of the people who had come up with the mumbo-jumbo; a momentary but expensive short-circuiting of his common-sense-motor that cost him the next round.

"What are managers supposed to be and do, Boss?" urged Dave, sounding somewhat impatient.

I caught his wink in the bar-side mirror. He really did want the message out and he knew it would have more impact coming from me that night than from him the following Monday. I cracked on.

"You mean, after all those fat salary checks I've been signing for you every month for the past 10 years, Dave, you still don't know what you're supposed to be doing? This certainly is an interesting development, and particularly so as you won't officially be taking the reins until next week. I might just need to have a word or two with the Chairman later about working out a Plan B over the weekend."

That comment of mine nearly led to the roof lifting off Molly's as I recall and it was Dave's turn for a bit of ribbing. I was only half-joking with him too. It might have been my last day, but neither he, nor anyone else, was going to put me out to pasture before I was ready to go. I mostly liked the guy, but he needed to be put back in his box every now and again; he was being a bit full-on with all his patronizing winking-in-the-mirror-buddy-buddy crap. I would get the message out in my time, not his, and his impatience – faux or otherwise – deserved a subtle slap down.

So, that is precisely what he got.

It's funny, I noticed too at the time how he glared at a few of the team who were laughing loudest at what I had said to him, taking names in his head, as he frequently did, like he was a member of the Thought Police or something. No matter how many times I told him over the years that he needed to lighten up a bit, he never could fully shake-off his uptight streak, just didn't seem to accept that he had a problem in that regard. It might be his Achilles' heel if he's not careful because nobody likes an anal name-taker.

When the laughter died down I tried to continue. "We're supposed to juggle and juggle well," I said. "That's what managers do."

"Hah, I totally knew we were working in a *goddam* circus," sneered Scott from over my left shoulder.

I remember thinking that he must have been waiting patiently for an opportunity to get a jibe in against the company; biding his time in the bushes like a cat waiting to pounce. Scott wasn't the happiest man on the planet and always could be relied upon to launch a scud missile onto proceedings at some point.

Normally, I had a rule that there was to be no bitching around the place, but nobody could chew on data like he could, so I made a call on it – kept him on board for his particular skill, but kept him out of harm's way for as much of the time as possible. And once he didn't whine too often, I could live with it. People always present you with tough choices of one sort or other.

"Nice try, Scott," I said, "what a surprise, you lasted more than an hour before getting a moan in. Watch out guys, it might start raining over there in a minute if you stand too close to him."

Even Scott laughed at that. The key, I had learned over the years, was not to indulge him, not to let him drag you to pity-city. And for the most part he lightened up; mostly he was a good guy.

Actually come to think of it, that's the way it is with the majority of people, I find. As the boss, it's vital not to let anyone else dictate the agenda in any shape or form. Take people where you want them to go, not where they might like you to go. Now don't get me wrong, that doesn't mean you end up treating them like sheep, or never listening to them – quite the opposite – but once the direction is collectively agreed, if certain parties don't want to come along, then they don't fit: nobody's fault, it's just life. If people aren't with you, then they're 'agin ya,' as George W once said, but I say it without the severe paranoia attached to how he meant it.

Anyway, I got back to trying to explain the juggling analogy.

"When I say juggle, I mean, that is precisely what managers must do. At its simplest, we juggle things. In fact, if you really want to know, once we have developed a clear vision for where we want the business to go, we need to juggle three things to get us there, three interdependent and sometimes competing things: the What, How and Who.

"First off but not necessarily in this order of importance, you have to worry about the 'What' – call it anything you like, but for me it's about strategy, goals, targets, financial results and other desired outcomes. In our business, you know that these targets include satisfying our customers, achieving profitability and making an acceptable return on investment. If we were a non-profit, that might vary slightly, but you get the picture. Results matter in any organization. And they always matter.

"Second up you have got to worry about the 'How' – the manner in which those results are achieved. That involves defining roles and responsibilities; planning and executing; managing key processes such as marketing and finance; using systems, tools and techniques to improve efficiency; and maintaining standards to name a few concerns. The goal in any business, as it is in ours, has to be to implement the best systems and create the right conditions to deliver the highest possible levels of productivity, efficiency and quality.

"Thirdly, as managers we have to focus completely on the 'Who' – by that I mean our people, which brings into play issues such as organization culture, teamwork, individual and group behaviors and applying effective leadership styles. We must get the best from our people by ensuring their commitment, competence and motivation. In my experience all the targets, systems and processes in the world are worthless, if the employees aren't prepared to really make them work. So, for me, our people have always been the priority because they ultimately deliver the results.

"That's how I see management anyway, and it certainly didn't do me any harm to keep it simple: simple but not simplistic, mind you. You have three primary areas of focus as a leader and they ain't one, two, three options. The trick is to constantly keep them balanced and aligned. That's where the juggling bit comes in. And I get sick and tired of everything about management being spiced up for effect – Chrissakes, it's damn simple: to manage you have to juggle."

"Jeez, take a drink there, Boss. You'll give yourself a heart attack," said Dave as I finished.

To be fair to him, he wasn't being sarcastic either when he said that. He was right. I had gone off on one. Even to the end, I was always passionate about stripping stuff back to the bare bones. Old habits die hard. But, strangely enough, the team actually was interested in what I was saying, or certainly most of them seemed to be, judging by the fact that the questions kept coming.

"And how in your experience, Boss, can we get that balancing act right?" asked Jane, one of the young stars in the firm, and someone whom I had long ago singled out as having the potential to achieve great things with us.

"As you likely know already, Jane, there's no simple answer to that: no secret, no 10 steps, no special sauce. But there is a basic equation to guide you that just never seems to get talked about today."

In full flow I drew it out as best I could on the back of a cocktail napkin and they passed it around.

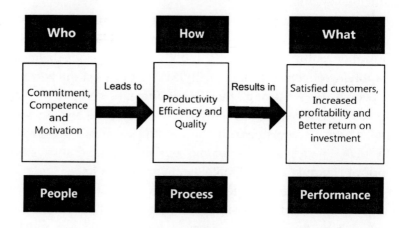

"Now for all of you who like fancy models – particularly you MBAs – then that bit of handiwork of mine doing the rounds at the moment won't have as many bells and whistles on it as some of the other frameworks you might have come across. But, trust me, it is just as effective in making the point.

"And it doesn't matter where you sit on the management ladder right now, or how long you have been sitting there, each of you who holds a position of authority in this business has some responsibility for balancing that equation, although how you do that in practice naturally depends upon the level involved. Here are a couple of examples of what I mean.

"Take Dave for instance, as the senior guy from now on, he may focus more on setting strategy and defining targets – the What – but he cannot ignore either the How or the Who.

"Equally, you Jane, as VP you contribute to defining the What of course, but you are also charged with execution – the How – and in doing so, you must engage your employees – the Who; and they need to buy into our vision if they are to really make a difference.

"Front line supervisors like you, Ray, hiding away at the back there, may devote a lot of attention on the ground to getting the job done to the right standard – the How – and this can only be achieved if you bring the best out of your team – the Who. Still, I think you'd agree, Ray, that you and your people also need broad familiarity with the big picture – the What – to be effective.

"So, that's your role as managers, you try to balance the three dimensions. And your success, at any level, is largely determined by how well you do it: 24 / 7 / 365. And there's no rule book to tell you how to go about it, just commonsense, the right personal qualities, some key skills and a bucket-load of experience. My one great pride and joy is that you all have, in my opinion, the right foundation to make good jugglers, or even better ones than you are already."

With the rant over, I stood to stretch my stiff leg and bought them all one last drink before Dave and I headed across Midtown to the Four Seasons.

There is no passion to be found playing small
– in settling for a life that is less than the one
you are capable of living.

Nelson Mandela

WDYDWYD?

Life went whizzing by.

The elderly man had just stepped down from the train and was steadying himself for a moment on the busy platform. As usual, it took him a while to adapt to all the to-ing and fro-ing. Out of the corner of his eye, he spied a quiet spot behind a pillar to his right and then, as if swimming against a shoal of humanity, he weaved his way to the calmness and placed his small suitcase on the ground.

In that welcome pool of tranquility, standing with his back to the pillar and holding his hands rigidly by his side, he began to stretch out his aching back – as his doctor had shown him how to do – by shifting his shoulders slightly upwards and gently moving his head up-and-down and from side-to-side. Then he began to raise himself up on his tippy-toes, or as close to that goal as the old legs would muster, whilst slowly moving his hands away from his body in a sort of flapping motion.

From a distance, he looked as if he was attempting to levitate, or for those under the influence of narcotics, to take-off in slow motion. At least, that's how it appeared to the two laughing teenagers on a nearby train who, using their cell phones, were now capturing the strange ritual unfolding before their glazed-eyes. *This is awesome grass, dude.*

As his head bobbed slowly up-and-down, then left-to-right, each movement lessening the pain, the aging man began to orient himself with the crowd around him and adjust to the faster pace of life. He didn't like big cities, loathed them in fact, but he never did miss his bi-annual trip to see his darling niece. She not only lived in the Big Apple, but was the big apple of his eye, the centre of the universe for an old bachelor who by circumstance or design never did find true love or have children of his own.

People said he was crazy to endure the long train ride from Charlotte when he could easily have made the trip in a few hours by plane. But what did people know anyway? Time, to his mind at least, was not lost on a longer journey, but found; every minute of the trip was enjoyable. He never did understand the modern obsession with rushing about.

Or the need to assault him with a suitcase when clearly he was not in the way.

The jolt brought him back to reality and he waited for an apology that never came. Rubbing his knee, he mumbled to himself: something about what might have happened had he been 20 years younger. Truth be known, a reversal of at least double that timeframe would have been required, if he was to have posed any real threat to the fast-disappearing offender.

Thoughts of the passage of time made him look at his watch. The Carolinian had arrived late and considering he would probably have trouble finding his niece's street, never mind her apartment – even though he had been there many times before – he should delay no longer, he thought.

Usually, well, for the past four visits to be precise, given what had happened on previous occasions, she had been there to meet him at Penn Station. But, on this day, she had explained that she could not make it; she was busy with something important at work that would push well into the evening. As she had long since given up trying to convince him to take a cab, she once more had provided him with the directions, more in hope than expectation of success.

He was not a senile man. Despite what some of his actions in the city might lead one to believe, that would be the wrong conclusion to draw. It was more a case that, try as he might, he just couldn't seem to fathom the maze that for him was any large urban area; the ability to find his way in unfamiliar places had been little better during his youth, so age was not the deciding factor here.

No matter how many times his niece had explained just how easy it was to find her apartment, or drew directions on a map for him, he never could get it right. If he didn't miss the correct subway stop, which unbelievably he had done twice previously, then he would likely take the wrong exit up to the street which would disorient him further. Often, he would venture East instead of West, or stray Uptown when Downtown was the logical direction. Each visit brought some new calamity of orientation, so the best that could be hoped for was that he would get within a block or two of where she lived. That of itself was considered an achievement by him and an enormous relief for her.

As it turned out, on this particular evening, he ended up doing what he had always done in the years before she took the initiative to collect him. When he couldn't find her place, as unsurprisingly was again the case, he located somewhere comfortable in what he believed to be the general vicinity and had a drink.

Then he gave her a call and she came as soon as she could.

When they did meet, though, it was always like seeing one another for the very first time. The joy, for both of them, was immense and as they were the only family each other had left in the world, this made the bond between them even stronger.

After the initial excitement subsided they settled into the same routine they followed every time he visited. The first evening, usually a Thursday, they would eat at home, often quite late if the train was delayed or if he had gotten badly lost. On Friday if she could not take the full day off, on her way to the office, she would bring him to the American Museum of Natural History on Central Park West where he never tired of spending a full day; and after she finished work, they would do whatever took their fancy.

On the Saturday if the weather was good, they would stroll around the city, or sit in the park under the sun, sharing ice creams, memories and an occasional tear. Dinner that night was always taken at the small Italian restaurant on her block and come Sunday morning, she would accompany him back to the station for his long journey home.

The visits were short and structured, but precious all the same.

Over the few days she would tell him all about her work, her life in the city and her loves, if there were any, which in fact there rarely were. She seemed totally engrossed in her career, something the old man believed was good in one sense, but seeing as time stood still for no one, worrying in another, although never once did he raise his concerns on the matter with her.

He, on the other hand, would bring her up to date with all the news from North Carolina – a task that never took very long for nothing much out of the ordinary ever happened.

This visit, during dinner at Luigi's, she explained that there had been some major changes in her company since he had last been in town, the previous CEO having retired a month or so before. "The big news is that I have just been promoted, basically to second-in-command," she said more or less out of the blue with characteristic understatement.

He shook his head and his eyes welled up with pride.

"And you waited until now to tell me? You are some girl, Janey, do you know that?" he said in pretend scold-mode, as he stood up, shuffled around the table and planted a big kiss on her cheek. Then he proceeded to embarrass her by ordering champagne and telling everyone within earshot that they were in the presence of greatness.

When they had toasted her success, she told him that she had also started a prestigious new Executive Development Program at City of New York University, or CNYU as she called it, which had been organized for her by the previous CEO before he left; three hours, two evenings a week for the rest of the year. This was, she explained, the reason why she couldn't collect him at the station when he arrived. "So, all in all, everything is looking up work-wise," she assured him.

It was then that she seemed to remember something. A flash of excitement sparkled in her faultless blue eyes and she searched impatiently in her handbag, biting her lip slightly as she always did when on a mission. After several moments, once the lipstick, cellphone, hairbrush, atomizer, tissues, pens and various other nondescript items had been fished out and then replaced, she found a piece of paper, smoothed it down and passed it across the table to him.

The old man fumbled for the glasses in his breast pocket and placed them on the bridge of his nose. Drawing the candle towards him for extra light, he looked closely at the paper.

"What do you think that means, Uncle Wills," she asked using the pet name she had for him since childhood.

"Now, let me see ..." he said, stalling for time because in truth he had not the faintest idea what it meant. Searching for a pattern of some sort, he could clearly see that there were a number of Ws, Ys, and Ds involved; and for an excited second or two, he wondered whether it might not be some sort of play on the word 'wedding.' But he quickly thought better of voicing that particular suggestion.

"Oh, I give up," he said, after what he felt was an acceptable period, adding mock frustration to his tone for effect.

Jane laughed and explained that it stood for *Why Do You Do What You Do?* It was, she said, part of her first project on the development program.

"And they gave you the whole week to answer that one question? Sure there is no work in that, Janey? What sort of course have they sent you on?" he asked jokingly. "You can answer it off the top of your head, can't you?"

"But you see, Uncle Wills, I can't find an answer. That's the problem. When we spoke about it in class on Thursday evening, I simply could not come up with anything meaningful that made sense to the others. Yes, I talked about all the things I had achieved so far, or the plans I had for my new position but they kept telling me that all I was explaining was my role – be that past, present or future. They were looking for the Why behind it all. It was so frustrating ... Uncle Wills, do you know why you do what you do?"

"Yes, of course I do, Janey."

"So, why do you do it then?"

"For the money. Why else?"

Jane looked at him cautiously for a moment on the off-chance that he might actually have been serious. Then, catching his eye, they both burst into laughter. Serving as a no-win-no-fee lawyer in a small farming community for the past 20 years – and one who rarely won a case at that – was a far from profitable venture.

"But, seriously, why do you do it?"

"Because, Janey, I want to help people. No more, no less than that. Most of the contingency lawyers I know look at the odds of winning a case before they consider taking it on. I only look into the person's eyes and, if they seem to me like they need but also deserve help, then I agree to represent them regardless of the likelihood of winning."

"But, you don't make any money, Uncle Wills, and you have had to work way past retirement age. How can that be rewarding?"

"I made all the money I needed for a good life long ago, Janey. I have plenty to get by, or as much as I need at any rate, which is not really a lot. Okay, you are right, none of the cases I take on these days make me much money, but they do make me happy. And that's far more valuable. I could retire any time I wanted to, really I could, but what would I do all day?

"Yes, it is true, I do lose more cases than I win nowadays although that's not because I'm suddenly a lousy lawyer, or that I am too old to do what I do well. No, I lose them because most of the cases are unwinnable anyway. Yet what I give my clients is the understanding that they are not alone, that they count. Both they, and I, get something from that, I believe.

"And even if I don't win I often raise awareness on certain issues or spark debate around town about important matters – that is an invaluable service to the community-at-large, I think.

"I don't know if your dear old dad ever told you this, Janey," he continued, "but when I finished law school, I graduated first in my class. Yes, I had offers from some of the top firms here and in Washington, DC but the big city life never appealed to me. I always said that, once I qualified, I would put my skills to good use in places where people still cared about one another. And that's what I did.

"Oh, don't get me wrong, I didn't always do it for charitable or civic reasons alone – but I made my money relatively early in life, and when I had enough put aside, I closed that practice and then started to do what I really wanted to do. Oh, for sure, my partner in the firm was absolutely furious with me at the time, and probably still is, but he went on to bigger and brighter things and was appointed to the bench a number of years back, so it worked out for him too in the end.

"Since I folded the business, I have spent my time helping those less fortunate than me. That's my Why, Janey. Simple as that."

"But, I don't feel anything remotely like those powerful motives in what I'm doing," she began, "even though it's all going very well for me right now. I just do what I do because I want to get on in life. There's no real Why for me in my job. That makes me a failure, doesn't it?"

"Far from it, Janey ... let me tell you a little story about someone you may have heard of that might help put your mind at ease. This man I am thinking of was a farmer for a while: hated it with a passion by all accounts. Then he was, at one time or another, a rail-splitter, boatman, storekeeper, postmaster and a surveyor. He even considered becoming a blacksmith at one point. He was also part-owner in a business that went bankrupt, although he didn't walk away from his debts. His life had many twists and turns until he found something that he was passionate about.

"And when he did find his thing, armed with his undoubted talents, he became very good at his chosen field. Even so, it still wasn't until his early 50s that he achieved his ultimate goal.

"Who do you suppose I am talking about, sweetie?"

"I have no idea, Uncle Wills. Who is it?"

"Abraham Lincoln ... you see, not everyone finds it easy to figure out what their passion in life is, or indeed to find it early, and he was no exception. But when he did find what he was looking for, he achieved great things. In fact, when he could answer your *WDYDWYD?* puzzle, nothing held him back.

"You'll find your Why in due course, Janey, and, by the way, it doesn't have to be as lofty an ambition as to become President. Each to his own. Keep thinking about it and, in time, it will come to you. That's how it works for most people. It will hit you when you least expect it to. The best people, in any walk of life, are the ones who at some stage or other find a Why that is all-consuming for them, one that drives them on to achieve great things, even if it doesn't always require them to seek great office or change the world.

"The problem is not that you can't find your Why right this minute, the real problem would be if you never cared about finding it in the first place ..."

*Our business is infested with idiots who try
to impress by using pretentious jargon.*

David Ogilvy

FRUITLESS DEBATES

Jack was old-school. But he was far from old-fashioned.

And he liked to talk leadership. Truth be known, it was one of his favorite topics, if only because he felt the need to fight back against what he liked to call the 'baloney brigade': those who talked a lot about the subject, but who wouldn't recognize real leadership if it walked up holding a sign and bit them on the ass.

As a successful and award-winning businessman, he had plenty to say on the matter too – in plain and simple terms – so he was in big demand as a speaker at various conferences and events. In some ways, he saw himself as a lone voice of reason holding back the tide of jargon and hyperbole. On occasion, he got so worked up about the need to call a spade a spade that his wife teased him that all he was missing was the tights and red cape.

It was therefore no surprise at all that, when the invitation to speak at the Young Managers Networking Event arrived on his desk some months earlier, he had quickly accepted. He rarely turned down an opportunity to gain some new converts to the cause.

Leaving Lakeville for the 100 mile or so trip down to the city, he began to think about what he was going to say in his talk later that evening. It wasn't so much a search for content, rather his main concern as he drove slowly out the long winding driveway was context. Like an artist, he wanted to mold and shape a message fit for the occasion. He didn't do standardized presentations.

Nor did he ever formally prepare his speeches – he much preferred to speak off-the-cuff – but that didn't mean he just turned up and tried to do it on-the-fly. No, the perfectionist in him simply wouldn't allow that. The two hour drive ahead was more than ample time for his speech to take shape.

In any case, as he pulled in to buy some gas, he already had a fair idea of how he wanted to begin. Whatever ground was to be covered during the talk, he would likely open by sharing his opinions on the 'not-so-great-debate', as he had christened it. Standing by the car whilst the tank filled with fuel, somewhat lost in the rhythmic *prring* of the pump, he thought again about just how much he hated the whole leadership *versus* management debate. Certainly no top-up on that front was necessary for him, because he had long ago had his fill of it.

It was, he believed, a complete and utter waste of time to debate the distinctions between leadership and management, a fruitless exercise that resulted in nothing but hot air and sore ears. It wasn't that he dismissed the subtle differences out of hand, clearly they were valid but in his experience, discussing the merits of each tended to throw up as many questions as answers.

He had seen many times over the years how significant time and energy were often wasted chasing down somewhat abstract concerns like: were management and leadership complementary, or mutually exclusive? Could a manager be a leader, or a leader a manager? Was leadership a function of management, or the other way around? So much baloney, he thought to himself, as he tapped every last dreg of gas from the nozzle. *Better in my tank than theirs.*

In fact, he found that once a group of people got going on questions such as those, it was hard to get them to stop; even harder to achieve consensus or to come to any meaningful conclusions from what he had seen. He never could fathom why some people sought to split leadership from management when the truth was they formed two sides of the one coin.

Settling back into his seat he knew then that he would begin by saying that he felt therefore the debate was best avoided, not simply as a convenient way of bypassing a thorny issue but perhaps he would stress, it was less important whether it was called management or leadership and infinitely more interesting what actually happened, or should happen, in practice. That's what he really believed. And he had plenty of evidence to back up that view.

Out there in real life, he knew plenty of 'managers' who were actually great leaders, others who were less so and then there were a few who got it consistently wrong. He also had the dubious honor over the years of meeting individuals with snappy titles such as 'leadership fellows' or 'emerging leaders,' some of whom had a distinctly annoying aura about them ... like they somehow believed that, because of their title, they were akin to emperors-in-waiting. No doubt, he thought as he pulled the shade down against the sun, many of those egotistical idiots are still doing just that: waiting.

For Jack, experience had taught him that whether an individual called themselves a manager or a leader and what specific title they held was essentially irrelevant; terminology was not really the issue, although at times it unfortunately became the focus of the debate. What really mattered most in daily business life was not what was on an individual's nameplate, but how they acted and behaved on a consistent basis.

Sure, at times, he knew very well that 'leading' took precedence, such as when setting overall direction for the business or when motivating and inspiring people but as far as he was concerned, process always had to be 'managed' in order to deliver the expected levels of performance. An individual could have any vision they wanted, or be blessed with a second-to-none ability to inspire others, but unless he could manage the day-to-day aspects of a business, then he would not be as successful as he might otherwise be.

Equally, someone might be great at managing execution, but if she could not motivate and inspire people to work together to achieve common goals, then that too would lead to some degree of ineffectiveness. Leading and managing, for him therefore, were joined at the hip and could not be separated.

As he turned onto the I-684 South about half-way through the journey, a solid platform upon which to build his speech had been shaped in his mind. He would address the not-so-great-debate, or more correctly, he would make the point that there was, in fact, no worthwhile debate because it wasn't a case of either-or.

He would then go on to explain how he genuinely believed that the term 'manaleader' would be a better tag to use, as it more closely reflected what was really required in daily corporate life. It was a far more accurate description of what was necessary than either the term 'manager' or 'leader'. But, he hated jargon so he would explain how he used the words leader and manager interchangeably with his own people, but always meant it strictly in the sense of a manaleader – someone with the ability to both manage and lead.

And being able to do both well, he would emphasize, actually required an individual to have the broad range of attributes and skills necessary to really engage their people in order to achieve the best results possible; no mean feat in itself because in his experience, only the most versatile of candidates could come close to harmonizing those often conflicting challenges.

Having said all that, he knew too that he also would have to reassure his relatively young audience that they didn't need to be supermen or women, extraordinary heroes or corporate champions, to be effective. He would make the point that managers were from Earth not Krypton, another favorite quip of his. But at the same time, he would tell them that they did need to be a cut above the rest if they wanted to stand out as real leaders and that their potential for lasting success would be down as much to who they were and how they thought because that ultimately determined what they did. Attitude drives behavior.

Not to intentionally deflate anyone's balloon he also would have to add that, unfortunately, he saw all too frequently how, in many businesses, individuals still were appointed to leadership positions, or retained existing posts, despite the fact that they clearly lacked the breadth of characteristics and skills necessary to manage and lead. His advice to his audience would be that, if they wanted to make it over the long term, they needed to constantly raise their personal capabilities so they could do both.

And do them consistently to a high standard.

The traffic worsened as he approached the outskirts of the city and his pace of progress slowed, at times almost to a crawl; the cars herded like motorized sheep into single-file lanes as a result of the road works. This strangely reminded him of a second bug-bear which he definitely wanted to address during his talk, that being how certain commentators portrayed work leaders as somewhat akin to messiahs who had 'followers' desperately longing to be shepherded to some form of organizational promised land.

He intensely disliked that image, mainly because he thought it was complete and utter BS. Even the thoughts of it made him dig his nails slightly into the steering wheel.

From his perspective, any leader who viewed his employees as followers didn't actually get what leading was all about in the first place. For sure, he was aware that his views went against the widely promoted image of leader as champion, but Jack didn't care. He lived in the real world and had seen the untold damage done by some of those corporate pied-pipers.

Yet in that world, he knew too that there were, for sure, great business leaders who possessed a messianic quality about them. He had met some of them over the years, although in truth such individuals formed the minority of a minority. Still, even with those really great managers he had encountered over his lifetime, he would never have 'followed' them as such.

Had he respected and admired them? Undoubtedly, he had.

Would he have worked his backside off for them? Hell, yes.

Would he have gone that extra mile for them? Absolutely, he would have done so.

But follow them? In a work setting ...?

No, sorry, he didn't think so. That analogy simply did not work for him and most people he knew thought exactly the same, because the truth was that the majority of employees today – at any level – were not looking to follow anyone. What they did want was for their boss to view them as partners, not drones who were willing to line up behind him like lemmings. Jack firmly believed that certain people needed to get real about the leader-follower drivel they promoted. He wouldn't pull any punches on that particular issue during his talk.

As he arrived on Broadway, in his mind, he took a step back and admired his work: words and themes had been skillfully structured and shaped to fit an occasion. The molding was complete. The speech was ready.

A shouting cabbie – his views on Jack's driving delivered in true Manhattan style – brought him quickly round. As he snapped to, he had a slight panic attack, as drivers often do when they have been deep in thought, because he could hardly remember any of the journey; it was as if he had somehow driven it on remote control. But, he had made it safely in the end, so no harm done, he thought to himself as he parked up and checked into his usual hotel on West 62nd.

He was raring to go.

L ater that evening, as he stood at the podium facing the large group of young managers, most seemingly in their mid to late 20s, he felt a bit old but invigorated at the same time. Tall and relatively fit for his age, with his shock of white hair and perfectly tailored suit, he had a commanding presence about him. As the host introduced him and ran down his list of achievements, he was reminded too that, many years previously, he had attended a similar event and how the speaker that night had left an indelible impression on him. He knew he had the potential to do the same for one or two of his audience.

With the introductions out of the way, he began.

"In November 1988 300 students from The Hart House Debating Club at the University of Toronto debated the interesting resolution that 'There is nothing not worth talking about' and managed to keep going at it for a very impressive 388 hours and 15 minutes. Having set a record for the longest running debate ever, a broken tape destroyed the evidence before it could be sent to the *Guinness Book of World Records* for verification."

He left his words hanging over the heads of the group, waiting for a reaction. Experience told him someone would respond if he paused long enough.

He wasn't to be disappointed.

"I don't get it," said one young man at the front. "What has that got to do with leadership?" he added, using that cocky tone that is, on occasion, an unfortunate by-product of the brashness of youth.

Jack smiled at the guy and, to those watching, he seemed for a moment to be contemplating his next move – as a trout eying the bait might do. He was fairly long in the tooth and should have known better than to let a young gun wind him up, but he always found it hard not to go toe-to-toe with someone who came out swinging. Jack laughed to himself as he thought how, even after all these years, he still had to hold back when someone waved a red flag at him, but he passed on the worm, for he had long ago learned how to keep his cool and, more importantly, why that was the best option.

Anyway, this guy was just out of short pants.

"The point to that story ...?" Jack replied a moment later. "Well, what it means is that some debates do prove fruitless in the end ..."

Nothing endures but personal qualities.

Walt Whitman

GREAT EXPECTATIONS

People can surprise and even astound you at times.

In a good way, I mean.

And in the process you end up thinking a whole lot less of yourself because you initially thought so little of them; the arrogance you pretend isn't there suddenly rises to the surface and bites you.

It happened to me recently.

I'm not proud of the fact, but there is no denying it.

Yes, even as a writer, with my supposedly finely tuned antennae towards other human beings, I was so far wide of the mark as to raise questions whether the radar was even switched on. Although I benefited greatly from the encounter I still feel a real sense of shame for underestimating the man. As much as he had risen beyond my expectations, I must surely have fallen way short of his.

I am truly pathetic at times.

I had spent the morning talking with groups of employees in order to gather information for a book I was working on. After a quick snack, I tried to settle down in the Mid-Manhattan Library on Fifth, supposedly for an afternoon of research and writing, but it wasn't to be. Inner Voice was having none of it.

It's coffee time, it's coffee time. Drop the work for today.

Eventually, there was no silencing him, so I just threw in the towel. Some days the words flow easy, others not at all. No point in flogging a dead horse.

I strolled around Midtown for a while and then decided to find somewhere to sit and send a few emails; if I couldn't write, then at least I would get some mundane tasks out of the way. As I passed a small bar Inner Voice was at it again.

This will do nicely.

Now I don't usually do bars in the afternoon and I certainly never drink until after five – well, mainly never – but the free Wi-Fi sign in the window was the clincher. Most spots you go these days you have to pay for it and as a struggling writer, cheap is my middle name.

The place was dead when I entered: no one there but the barman and I.

Bar stool or banquette, bar stool or banquette.

I chose the stool.

"Good afternoon, sir, what can I get you?" he asked as I sat down.

"Just a coffee, thanks," I said.

He didn't offer me a choice, there was just one type of brew going. My kinda place.

He was short and stocky. The barman, I mean. And he clearly had a bit of mileage on the clock. For some reason, he sort of reminded me of an aging Jesuit I once had as a teacher. What was it we used to call him? Ah yes, Stumpy Stevens, that was it. Anyway, the barman's pleasant round face reminded me of that priest. Watching him prepare the coffee, he seemed like a gentle, trusting sort, although his upper arms and chest forewarned you that he could still have a fair go at strong-arming you out the door if the need arose.

"There you are, sir. Would you like anything with that? Some cookies, or a slice of pie, perhaps? We got ..."

"No thanks. Just the coffee is good." And off he went about his business.

I sat back on the swiveling stool, turning slowly from side-to-side as I took in the surroundings. Some 'old' bars can be full of fake memorabilia and replica sepia-toned photographs of days gone by but, to be honest, this place seemed like the real deal.

It had a beat-up look about it.

"That's me in the photo up there beside the mirror. Third from left, when I had a full head of hair, of course," he said laughing as he placed a tray of glasses down on the counter. "Yeah, been here for almost 30 years now, seen a hell of a lot of change around this neighborhood in that time, I can tell you. Oh boy, has it changed."

Don't go there. You don't want to get sucked into strolling down memory lane with this dude.

"I'll bet it has," I said as I flipped open the lid on the laptop; sort of like hanging out the do-not-disturb sign. I booted up and got connected.

"And what kind of business are you in yourself, sir?" he asked a moment later, apparently none too good at reading the signals for someone with his Pearl Anniversary in the bar trade approaching.

The kind of business that's none of yours.

"I write for a living," I said in as non-committal a tone as I could muster without seeming completely rude and obnoxious.

"Oh ... it-was-a-dark-night-as-Mickey-hit-the-mean-streets kind of writer, or the sort who writes computer code and speaks in a language nobody understands?"

"It's not the latter, that's for sure," I replied, trying very hard not to be lured in.

"Yea, I didn't think so, seeing as you seem to have a personality. So, what sort of books is it, sir? Mystery novels, sci-fi, or what?"

He was getting me to nibble. I had to give him that. "I mostly write business books but I cover other issues as well, like a good human interest story if one comes along."

"Really ...? You're not Stephen Covey by any chance, are you?"

No, I can count past seven.

Inner Voice is a bitter sort at times and naturally I didn't express that last sentence out loud. Had I done so, I also would have had to add that I don't sell books by the shed-load either. "No, I'm not him. Why do you ask?"

First question fool. He wins. He has you hooked now.

"Well, if you had been him, I would have asked you for my money back. I read that *7 Habits* stuff a few years back – did all that was suggested, and more – but I'm still stuck here serving beers for a living."

We both laughed at that. I closed the lid on the laptop.

It's good to talk sometimes.

"So, what type of business books do you write?" he asked.

"I write about work, about organizations, about people, about people and their work and about leaders too. I write about how it all fits together. You might say that I'm less worried with the 'how to' and more interested in the 'why' part."

He looked at me as if I had two heads.

I could see from the puzzled look on his face that he must have been wondering whether I hadn't actually been lying about writing code; either that, or he took me for an ex-lush on the wagon with nothing better to do of an afternoon than impersonating a writer. I had another go at explaining what I do.

"For example," I said, "the book I am writing at the moment is about employees and their bosses and particularly what it is that people look for in a good manager."

"And how's that working out for you?" he enquired only slightly more reassured by the sound of it.

"Today was a struggle to be truthful ... actually I'm sort of stuck on it period, have hit the wall: writer's block, you might say. I've done the research but it's just not coming together at all well, can't seem to put what I want to say into words that make any sense."

"Anyways, if you ever need any advice on the subject, just let me know. I'd be happy to help."

Yeah, that's just what we need: a barman's opinion. That'll help us past the block.

"Sure, thanks for the offer. I'll keep it in mind."

"No, I'm serious," he said.

You could tell by the sudden change in tone that he had taken offence at the brush off. I felt like a real jerk at that point.

"Night after night," he continued, "I listen to bosses sitting at this bar talking about their employees and *vice versa*. You see, most of our weekday trade here is the after-work crowd so trust me, if there is one thing I do know about, it's how people feel towards each other in a work context."

I felt beyond bad when he said that.

"So, what would you say it is that employees look for in their leaders, from what you hear your customers saying?" I thought I'd throw him a little bone to make him feel good, or more likely, to make myself feel better.

"Hmm, let me see," he said as he started to polish a glass. "From what I can tell having listened to people over the years, I don't think you can say there is just one thing – and everybody has their own individual needs of course – but there are common qualities that people look for in their bosses which seem to shift in order of importance as times change.

"To me, everything on that list combines to show employees that their boss respects them, which is really what people are searching for, don't you agree?" he asked without actually waiting for an answer.

"Extra, extra, read all about it," he continued, suddenly morphing into a somewhat bizarre pretend-newsboy whilst pacing up and down waving his cloth in the air, "amazing discovery made, incredible news today folks, read all about it, people want to be respected by their bosses, city in shock ..." He ended his odd impression with a laugh before continuing his train of thought, thankfully in his normal voice again.

"Everyone I have ever listened to talking about their manager says, at some point in the conversation, that they want to feel respected. But no one thing on its own will achieve that. Hence the list."

"And what would you say is top of that list right now?" I asked, tossing another treat.

"Well, they have always been important but, given all that has happened over the last few years, I think honesty and integrity have jumped to the top of the pile. People seem to be tired of all the BS and just want their bosses, at any level, and in any context, to be upfront with them. At least, that's what I'm hearing more often around the bar today: stop the cloak and dagger stuff, forget about pretending that you're God's gift to leadership and just be upfront with us. Respect us enough not to lie to us or treat us like morons. That's what seems to be big on the wish-list at present, or so the folks who come in here tell me."

I discreetly took out my scratch pad and placed it on the counter. As I opened the cover, my pen rolled down the page and fell to the floor: settling amongst my misconceptions. This guy was spot-on in what he had said because that was one of the main messages I was getting from all the focus groups of employees that I had held.

Stooping to pick up the pen, I felt a weight of shame on my shoulders.

"Actually," he said, "I was only last week talking to a guy about the integrity issue and he reminded me of a funny story that happened to Hillary Clinton on the campaign trail for the Presidency back in '08. She apparently stated during one interview that, as First Lady in 1996, she had landed in Bosnia under sniper fire and had to run with her head down to get into a car to avoid being shot. I think she was trying to bump up her 'who-do-you-want-answering-that-phone-in-the–Oval-Office-at-3-in-the-morning' credentials by saying that.

"Anyways, as it turned out, some hack – clearly with too much time on his hands – later found old news video footage of the event which showed that she had actually arrived without incident, accompanied by her 15-year-old daughter Chelsea, the comedian Sinbad and singer Sheryl Crow. Her handlers had to admit that she 'misspoke' about the incident.

"The guy who told me the story said that Sinbad later used the incident in his routines and said stuff like: 'What kind of President would say, *Hey, man, I can't go 'cause I might get shot so I'm going to send my wife and daughter ... oh ... and take a guitar player and a comedian with you.*"

We both laughed at the preposterous image.

"Now, don't get me wrong," he continued, "I'm a big fan of Hillary so I'm not saying she's dishonest – how would I know – but the point I want to draw from the story is that people expect complete honesty today. It's jumped up the list – big time. Telling the odd little porky, or 'misspeaking' is one thing, but lacking values and integrity when you are in charge of others, at any level, is quite another matter entirely.

"I'm sure you'll agree," he added, "we all make allowances for the occasional massaging of the truth – most customers who come in here tell me, when the subject comes up, how they understand that their boss can't always tell them exactly what's going on – but an absence of values or lack of integrity is completely different and is no longer acceptable. Or, that's what I'm being told at least."

He was right. He really was. "And what else would be on your list from what you have heard customers saying over the years?"

He picked up another glass and raised it to the light, holding it there momentarily as if the answer to my question was somehow projected onto it. He then began to twirl it in his cloth. Looking over at me, he answered.

"One point that comes up quite a lot is how people seem to want their boss to have a sense of where they are headed as an organization, or as a team. I know that there was a lot of talk in business circles about 'vision' over the past decade – believe you me, plenty of people used to mock their company's vision in here after they'd had a few drinks – but I still hear my customers talking about how they want their boss to be forward-looking and to have a realistic plan in place for how to get there.

"There's nothing worse, it would seem, than a leader who has – what I've heard a few people in here call – a 'headless chicken' approach, where there is no direction, or when it changes from one day to the next."

This was all great stuff. In his own words, he was confirming what I was hearing and more to the point, he was describing it in easy to understand terms. *Hey loser, he should be writing the book, not you.* "What else would you say is important?" I asked, trying to ignore Inner Voice.

"Well, one of the bigger discussions I have heard about leadership over the years is whether employees want, or expect, their boss to be charismatic. Certainly, there have been some pretty heated arguments in here on more than one occasion about that issue. What I can tell you for certain is that nobody wants to work for what they call around here, a 'wet fish', a boss who brings you down rather than up. But at the same time, some managers who think they are charismatic are really just full of ... well, you know what I mean.

"And we get plenty of those creeps in here," he continued "the finger-clicking crowd as I call them. I've happily thrown more than a few of those assholes out the door for their click-clicking.

"Anyways it seems to me that people want to work for someone who can inspire them but not necessarily because they ooze charisma, chant meaningless slogans or whoop-and-holler a lot. No, what I hear people saying is that they can be inspired in many different ways: by bold action, by consistency in behavior, by calmness in a crisis and by powerful ideas to name but a few ways.

"Sure, it would appear that a bit of charisma, when genuine, is welcomed but not necessarily a must-have as regards what people look for in their leaders. As well as that, people seem to want their boss to have a real sense of passion and an upbeat attitude to keep everyone on board.

"Now," he said, and I sensed a slight change in his tone, "I have really seen the importance of having a positive mindset from my own nephew Karl. He's some guy, I have to tell you and he is making a big name for himself with his own company just a few blocks from here. Despite a pretty major health scare in the past couple of years, he's managed to stay really positive about things, always looking ahead, forever finding the good in the bad; and it seems to really rub off on others around him. When he comes in here with his team, which he does every now and again, you can see how they all look up to him and like being around him."

There was a quiet moment as a thought seemed to linger in his mind.

He was again hitting the nail on the head. The feedback from the focus groups was saying similar things to me about charisma and positive mindsets. In fact a lot of employees I had interviewed felt that some lousy leaders they knew had equated charisma with arrogance, which was not what they were looking for at all. Equally, everyone I spoke with wanted an upbeat boss who had a positive outlook on life. This was turning into a very productive afternoon, I remember thinking.

When he appeared to have come through his moment of reflection I picked it up again. "And what else would be on the list from what you've heard your customers saying?"

"How long you got, bud?" he said smiling. "There's a whole heap of basic things you hear people complaining about when their boss lacks them. I mentioned earlier about consistency with regard to direction, but nothing seems to annoy people more than if their boss is inconsistent in action or behavior – the frustration of working for a manager from whom they didn't know what to expect from one day to the next has driven a fair few employees to drink, I can tell you.

"Another big issue is self-control, or more specifically, the lack of it. Over the years, I have heard so many people sit at this bar and tell me how they completely disrespect their boss because he, or she, lacks self-control and particularly if they are aggressive characters. As one guy said to me a couple of months back about his snappy and hostile manager, 'Who the hell would relish the thoughts of going to work to sit near a ticking time-bomb all day?'

"A related aspect that gets brought up around the bar quite frequently," he continued, "is that although people most certainly don't want their bosses to be bullies, they do want them to be assertive characters who have a backbone and are prepared to front-up when required. They want them to have *cojones* as they say, and to be brave and courageous in the decisions they take. Nothing, it would seem, from what I hear at least, is worse than working for a spineless boss who avoids difficult issues, sits on the fence or shifts positions to suit whichever way the wind is blowing."

He placed another sparkling glass down on the counter and went silent again for a while. He seemed more melancholy than before but maybe I was wrong about that too. My track record of judging this guy had been pretty dismal up to that point.

"Oh, I had nearly forgotten this one," he said suddenly, "but I think empathy is another big factor that employees look for, comes up time and time again. It never ceases to amaze me that in this day-and-age you should have to tell any manager that empathy is important but, from what I hear night after night, some bosses still seem clueless as to where other people are coming from, or they show a complete lack of concern for their employees.

"I'm not kidding about this either and, worse still, I have frequently listened in total shock at how some of them appear to have a really perverted sense of how to get the best out of others. Come to think of it, where is that article now ..."

Placing the glass on the counter and flicking the cloth over his shoulder, he began to rummage around in a drawer underneath the cash register. After a few moments, he turned and handed me a well-worn newspaper clipping. "Read this," he said, shaking his head.

I read through the article which, believe it or not, told a supposedly true story about how a manager in a company in Utah had water-boarded one of his employees during an outdoor teambuilding event in an attempt to highlight for the other employees present that they should work as hard at making sales as this particular employee had worked to breathe!

"Now I know what you're thinking," he said as I handed back the article, "for sure, it is an extreme example, given to me by one of my regulars and unlike that slightly psycho boss, most managers don't need to be told that people probably won't take too kindly to being water-boarded under any circumstances. But that doesn't mean I don't still hear unbelievable stories about how certain bosses remain completely oblivious to the needs and feelings of others.

"Actually," he continued, "there is one young woman who comes in here every now and again, a really lovely gal – what's her name ... Heather, yes, I think that's it. Anyways, she once described to me what you could only say was a catalogue of abuse she was suffering every day from her manager: constant sarcasm and snide remarks, aggressive attacks on her in front of others, unnecessary complaints about her work just to show her who was in charge – the whole nine yards of nastiness by all accounts.

"She told me one night, almost in tears might I add, that despite all of that crap, what got to her most was the deep sense of helplessness, that and the loss of self-esteem she was suffering due to the way her boss was treating her. The last I heard was that she had managed to find a new job so at least she got away from that nightmare.

"Now I don't know about you, sir, but I just cannot understand how one human being can willfully make life so miserable for another. It's simply beyond me," he said and I could see his neck muscles tense slightly as he thought about it.

Silence prevailed as we both struggled to erase water-boarding and bullying images from our minds.

In the quiet, I began to think about the alter-ego of leadership – the Mr. Hyde to Dr. Jekyll's pleasant façade – which seemed to get so little attention; all the noise was about the great leaders out there supposedly doing extraordinary things. For sure, there are many top managers around – no denying that – but a not insignificant number of the employees that I had come across during my research had highlighted that the daily reality of working for some so-called leaders was not such an uplifting experience.

I was reminded too of a study I had read called 'Bad bosses can damage your health' undertaken by a Swedish team of researchers. They found a strong link between poor leadership and the risk of serious heart disease and heart attacks among more than 3,000 employed men. The irony was not lost on me how it is that when some people say things like 'my boss makes me sick', turns out, or at least according to that study, they sadly aren't exaggerating.

As I made my way out front for a smoke, the health warning on my cigarette pack caught my eye.

Maybe it's time to start labeling bad bosses.

W hen I returned, I picked up on our conversation by asking the bartender what other issues his customers regularly brought up in relation to what they want from their leaders?

He looked at me sort of blankly for a moment before responding.

"Another point I hear people saying quite often is that they hate working for a boss who is too controlling, or what seems to be the popular way of describing it these days, someone who 'micro-manages' them to death. People seem to prefer a manager who allows them a bit of freedom in what they do. Linked to that is the idea of having a confident boss who is not afraid to release control generally and involve their employees in decision-making.

"Actually, while we're on the subject of how decisions are taken, one of the most common gripes I hear around this bar is when people feel their boss doesn't make an effort to consult, or fails to communicate with them on an ongoing basis. I don't think people expect to get their way on everything, but they do, as a minimum, want to have their concerns listened to and acknowledged. So, having a boss who is open to meaningful contact with his or her employees seems to be important."

I had to admit that this guy really did know people and work life, which I suppose shouldn't have been all that much of a surprise, given that his customers have probably off-loaded on him about the matter for many years. He offered me a refill of coffee and then I asked him had he any further insights to share.

"I would say that, as well as all the people-orientated stuff that people look for in their bosses, at the end of the day, they also want them to be competent and intelligent. That doesn't mean they expect their boss to have the highest IQ in the building because, as one customer said to me, the brightest people often cannot really relate to others due to the nerd factor.

"Yet, the best managers, or the ones that get talked about most around here at any rate, seem to be smart characters who benefit from having different forms of intelligence: the capacity to analyze and solve problems, knowledge related to the requirements of their job or an ability to be creative. Added to that, they always seem to have a fair helping of that critical, if somewhat intangible, commodity called commonsense.

"Actually, a related point is that people always tell me that they like to work for a boss who is not afraid to try new things, but that does not necessarily mean that they expect him or her to have all the answers; it's more a case that they create an environment where suggestions are welcomed from employees, so the flow of new ideas is encouraged throughout the business."

As he placed the final glass on the shelf another customer entered the bar.

"Hey Bob, what a hell-of-a-day I've just had. You have no freakin' idea! The usual, please. No, actually, make that a double. Boy, do I need it this evening. You won't believe the kind of day I just had ..."

When he had served the new entrant, Bob, as I then knew him to be, approached me to say that he had, as far as his memory served him, highlighted the most common points raised with him about what people wanted from their bosses. He didn't pretend it was the full list, but they certainly were the main things that he had repeatedly heard.

"Listen, thank you very much for the great insights, Bob," I said, "it's been more than helpful. And, can I just say that, *eh*, that I am, *eh*, I mean for earlier on ... that I am very, very ..."

"No need to say it, sir. I understand. You probably assumed that all I knew about was serving drinks, right? Don't worry on that score. Lots of people make that same mistake. Although, now that you bring it up, it reminds me of another good point for inclusion in your book," he said smiling. "People like bosses who are tolerant, who don't rush to judgment, but rather give everyone a chance to shine ...

"For what it's worth, sir, I'm here by choice, not because there weren't many other career alternatives that I could have pursued. Hey, I own the damn place, plus a couple more out in Queens too ... well, you have a nice evening, sir, and good luck with the book."

Those last comments of his went through me like a knife. He was right to say them too. I had been a condescending fool.

"Thank you, Bob," I said shaking his hand, "and I promise that I'll be back for a chat soon. And when the book is finished you'll get a big acknowledgement for all your help. See you soon. Bye."

"Goodbye, sir, and thanks again. There'll always be a warm welcome – and an open mind – waiting for you here at Molly's ..."

He winked as the knife turned.

When I got back to my apartment that evening I reflected on what Bob had said – taking the personal lesson on board – but also trying to match his comments with what my own research was saying about the characteristics people look for in their leaders. Thanks to the simplicity of his explanations of what customers had told him, I felt I was starting to push beyond the mental block. The book was taking better shape as a result of our chat.

As I worked it also struck me how it is that people still seem to underestimate the importance of the manager-employee relationship. One extract I found online from a study by Brad

Gilbreath, a researcher at Indiana University-Purdue University, really hit home just how important that dynamic is. He found that 'a worker's relationship with the boss was almost equal to his relationship with his spouse when it comes to the impact on his well-being. A rewarding job or even good rapport with co-workers cannot compensate for a negative relationship with the boss.'

Frightening really, although not all that surprising when you consider that a boss directly influences the pattern of an employee's life for over 2,000 hours in any given year. People get to choose their partners, not so their bosses.

The great thing about the Web is that there is not just serious stuff to be found online that can help reinforce a message. That night, I also came across a funny incident, which made me laugh but helped to highlight another important point for me that can often be overlooked when we talk about what people expect from their leaders. I located it on the social news website Digg under the headline, *Why you shouldn't have your boss on Facebook.*

It went something like this.

One evening after work, a girl named Lindsay posted the following tirade on her Facebook Wall (expletives deleted) against her boss, a man called Brian:

OMG I hate my job!! My boss is a total pervy ****, always making me do **** stuff just to **** me off.

Shortly later her boss, Brian, replied:

Hi Lindsay, I guess you forgot about adding me on here? Firstly don't flatter yourself. Secondly you've worked here five months and didn't work out that I'm gay? Thirdly that **** stuff is called your 'job,' you know what I pay you to do. But the fact that you seem to be able to **** up the simplest of tasks might contribute to how you feel about it. And lastly you also seem to have forgotten that you have two weeks remaining on your six-month trial period. Don't bother coming in tomorrow. I'll pop your P45 ['pink slip'] in the post and you can come in whenever you like to pick up any stuff you've left here. And yes, I'm serious.

A great story for inclusion in the book, I thought, and it did help to make the point that there is just no pleasing certain employees. No matter how good a manager is, he will never keep everyone happy; you just cannot win with some people. At times leaders do make easy targets for criticism; when it comes to the blame game they are like sitting ducks, the proverbial fish in a barrel you might even say. So, trying to keep all employees happy, all of the time, is simply not possible and, in reality, it is one of the few times when aiming for 100% is probably not a viable target for a leader.

A few days later as I worked on drafting the conclusion to my book, I tried to emphasize that all that any manager can do is their best but at the same time, they must have the right foundation in place to help them live up to the common expectations of employees. And with Bob's help, I was confident that the book offered the reader a good list of the leadership qualities that captured what people sought as priorities.

As I looked down through the list in front of me, I remember being struck by something important. I realized that, although management thinking is constantly evolving and changing, what people expect from their leaders remains largely the same over the long term, even if the order of priorities might shift. Why? Because it is a fundamental human need to feel valued and respected and, when a leader has the right mix of qualities on this list, they are better placed to deliver on that expectation.

For all its challenges, some aspects of management are not rocket science.

Some cause happiness wherever they go;
others, whenever they go.

Oscar Wilde

IT'S NOT ALL IN THE GENES

"Ayumu seemed to really enjoy his moment in the limelight. Well, it would appear so if the big smile he had on his face after the event was anything to go by ..."

The assembled mid-career executives sat watching the TV monitor as the narrator continued to describe an unusual event.

"In a televised head-to-head contest in 2008 which involved remembering the position of numbers on a screen the seven-year-old male chimp, raised in captivity, actually did three times better than Ben Pridmore, the world memory champion. This was not a minor achievement for Ayumu when you consider that one of Ben's particular talents is memorizing the sequence of a shuffled pack of cards in under 30 seconds!"

There were baffled glances between some of the group as to what this had to do with a class on leadership, although they had little choice but to stay tuned as the narrator provided more details.

"In the test, digits were shown on the screen for just one-fifth of a second and then hidden by white squares. The two unlikely contestants had to touch the squares in the order that the numbers had appeared. Ayumu got it right an amazing 90% of the time whereas poor old Ben scored a comparatively miserable 33%. Afterwards Ben took a fair bit of stick in the media about being chumped by a chimp in the man-ape match up and, as he said himself, 'I'd rather not be seen on TV doing worse than a chimpanzee in a memory test. I'll never live it down.' Certainly, the memory man will not forget the encounter, that's for sure ..."

Professor de Vreys, Head of Executive Development at CNYU, strode confidently to the front of the hall and switched the monitor off. He turned to face the participants, paused a moment, then smiled. "So, would anyone care to tell me what lessons might be drawn from that little episode?"

There was an awkward silence. Then, one participant spoke up.

"Yes, it means we should be looking more closely at who we hire in our finance departments ... the hairier the better by all accounts."

That got a muted laugh from a few in the room, but not the Professor. He wasn't what you might call the frivolous type. Under a disapproving glare, the comedian retrieved his lead balloon and slumped down into his seat.

"Does anyone else have something more age-appropriate to contribute?" asked the Professor.

He was again met by silence.

This was generally the reaction he received when he showed that video clip and asked that question. Truth be known, he wasn't really expecting an answer, rather he just wanted them to forget about their working day and focus on that evening's class. He used the video as a sort of mental bridge from the outside world to the theme of the session ahead.

He continued.

"Ladies and gentlemen, it is well known that chimpanzees share a large proportion of their DNA with us. They are undoubtedly our close relatives and, as you have just seen, in some ways they obviously manage to outdo us. Yet, despite the shared genes and his penchant for numbers it is highly improbable that Ayumu would be mistaken for Ben in a police lineup because similar does not necessarily mean the same. This analogy, I find, applies equally well to the management arena.

"Although all leaders do of course share a similar genetic make-up, they are most definitely not all the same; some truly excel in the role, whilst others simply fail to cut it. Naturally you cannot tell the good from bad just by looking at them, but spend time in the company of each and their talents and shortcomings as leaders will quickly emerge. In the leadership lineup there are real leaders and then there is ... well, shall we say, then there is the rest of the pack.

"Separating the wheat from the chaff when it comes to managers, though, is no easy task," the Professor continued, "as clearly none of them get it all right, or indeed all wrong. Every leader's performance is subject to peaks and troughs of some kind and we all have our good and bad days; some more bad than good, unfortunately. But when judged over the long term I have seen how certain leaders continually outperform others, and at times, by a significant margin.

"The purpose of this evening's class is to explore this gap in leader performance. In a few moments you will use your past experiences to help you to identify and classify the various manager-types you have encountered. In your appointed groups, you will be asked to differentiate between the Good, the Bad and, just to be confrontational, let's call the last lot, the downright Nasty leaders you have come across in your careers to date.

"However, to be in a position to make those distinctions, you will need some sort of framework to guide your efforts, some means of defining what leaders should do and from that, you can separate the winners from losers."

He tapped the return key on his laptop and a slide appeared on the screen.

Engage	Engaging *People* to ensure their commitment, competence and motivation	The 'leading' part
Achieve	Harnessing that engagement by focusing on *Process* to ensure productivity, efficiency and quality, in order to achieve the *Performance* and results required.	The 'managing' part

"Leaders," he continued, "as you undoubtedly already know, are concerned with three important dimensions of work: performance, process and people. To be effective, they must engage their people in order to achieve outstanding results and they must do it consistently over the long term. In other words, they must lead and manage well.

"Using this basic engage-to-achieve concept, I would like you to define the different types of managers you have encountered in the past, based on how well they coped with this interrelationship. Apply any descriptor tags you like but try to give us a real flavor as to what it is that each leader-type does or does not do to warrant the label you give them. In other words, paint some mental pictures for us.

"However, in doing so, please understand that I am not asking you for personality profiles of leaders – that is impossible, for each is different naturally – but rather try to group them according to their common behavior patterns."

He then divided the class into three groups. Jane was allocated into the team looking at the Good leaders, with a second group examining the Bad and a third identifying the Nasty types.

As is always the case with group activities, and particularly so after a hard day's work, it was a real struggle to get going. Slowly but surely, though, each of the groups warmed to the task and through sharing their experiences, began to broadly classify the various types of leaders they had met in their nominated categories. As they worked Professor de Vreys spent time sitting in turn with the teams, observing how they operated as a unit, the contributions each individual made and generally the quality of the discussions.

When the allotted time for the exercise had elapsed, he signaled to all teams that one person should be appointed to present the findings.

"I have observed and listened with interest to your work," he said, "and I am not sure whether it was those who were looking for the Good leaders, or the group searching for the Nasty types that had more fun, or indeed the easier task. Anyway, all shall be revealed.

"Let us begin with the Good examples as it always makes sense to start with a positive rather than a negative benchmark."

Jane was nominated to present the findings from her group, or suckered into it more likely, she thought as she approached the front of the hall. She turned to face the class and began with a question.

"Does anyone remember who won the Men's 100m final at the Beijing Olympics?"

The audience replied quite quickly that it was Usain Bolt.

"Do you know who posted the slowest time in the heats?" she followed up, to which of course there was no response.

Actually, unbeknownst to her, the comedian from earlier had contemplated throwing out some obscure Chinese name to frustrate her efforts at grabbing the audience's attention, but then thought better of it; he really did need to shake off the back-to-school mentality, he thought to himself, as he tried to concentrate on what she was saying.

Jane continued.

"Every field of human endeavor has its high achievers, the elite, those who deserve recognition for their excellence," she explained, "and our team has coined the term 'Genuine Leaders' to represent the best leaders we have encountered in our working lives. Genuine Leaders, we believe, are the chosen few, they excel in the role, are a step above other managers and are the very best that any organization has to offer, serving as examples for others in terms of their attitudes, attributes and actions.

"Okay, don't get me wrong, we are NOT saying that they are perfect or infallible by any stretch of the imagination, but they do consistently perform to a high standard and they deserve recognition for that fact."

Jane was a good speaker and she could sense that she was holding the attention of the class.

"Naturally not all Genuine Leaders are the same and there is no mold or template to describe one; they are individual characters with different personalities. What we believe, though, is common to them all is their talent for engaging and achieving and, in doing so, they successfully balance the three dimensions of work: people, process and performance. When we discussed the types we have met over the years, we felt there were actually two categories of Genuine Leaders to be found: 'Nurturers' and 'Stars'.

"Nurturers," she went on to say, "form the majority of the Genuine Leaders in our experience. Now on first hearing this description, you could be forgiven for thinking that we are promoting these leaders as some sort of 'mother-hens' but that is not the case at all. Yes, Nurturers are balanced and team oriented individuals who show real concern for the well-being of their employees; they truly value their people. But when you interact with them, you also quickly notice that these managers are very determined to achieve high quality results and are never prepared to accept second best or shoddy performance.

"So, they do like to help their people grow and develop, but they also expect a lot in return.

"Although not necessarily the most inspirational of managers Nurturers engage others through their strength of character, warm personalities and the positive relationships they build with them. Nurturers are not afraid to empower their people either and to provide them with appropriate levels of autonomy, depending upon the circumstances involved. Employees respond well to these leaders simply because, in words that we have heard expressed many times, they feel valued and respected as human beings.

"Yet, for all of this, these leaders expect their people to deliver on expectations. They do not tolerate underperformance, are prepared to confront it head on, but when doing so they seem capable of getting their point across without having to resort to aggressive behaviors. Employees quickly recognize when they have stepped over the line and are given ample opportunities to improve, with appropriate support when required.

"However we have all seen examples in the past where Nurturers showed that they would not be taken for fools under any circumstances and those who consistently fail to deliver are not endured for long because these leaders recognize that to do so only affects the productivity and motivation of others. In that sense, they are most definitely not mother-hens."

She paused briefly to let that last sentence sink in.

"The second category of Genuine Leader we had encountered were what we called Stars. This type of leader is always in the minority within organizations, we believe, because they are the truly exceptional leaders. None of us came across them very often – some never had – but when we did, they stood out a mile. They have the same desire to engage with their teams as Nurturers do but, in our experience, what sets them apart is that they also possess a strongly inspirational quality about them. They are those special few individuals who have a natural gift of being able to really lift employees, in a real, meaningful and authentic way.

"So to conclude," she said, in wrapping up, "we feel that working for both types of Genuine Leaders is a deeply enriching experience most of the time because they create a work environment based on partnership and mutual achievement. Certainly, from our experience, the morale, motivation and levels of engagement that we have felt ourselves, and seen amongst other employees, when working for these managers is always impressive.

"Thank you for listening."

Professor de Vreys was evidently impressed by the work of Jane's group and proceeded to expand on some of the points raised about effective leadership. Having drawn out these key learning points he handed over the floor to the spokesperson for the second group – a guy called Mike – who proceeded to explain their findings as regards Bad Leaders.

He began in somewhat unusual fashion.

"There have been many interesting and indeed bizarre impostors throughout history," Mike said to slightly puzzled looks from the floor.

He then proceeded to tell a story about a notorious Count Victor Lustig who plied his deceptive trade in the early 1900s. As a conman, he apparently excelled in its dark arts and, whilst he may have started on a small scale, he eventually worked his way up to one of the most famous scams of all time: that of selling the Eiffel Tower to a naïve scrap metal dealer whilst posing as a French government official. A truly remarkable achievement Mike thought everyone would agree.

"Just like any fraudster or scam artist," he added, "our group believes that certain so-called leaders are pretending to be something they are not. Sure, they might be masquerading as Genuine Leaders, as the first group aptly called them, but for most of the time they are something else entirely. We believe, again from our practical experience, that there are leaders out there who, whilst not necessarily bad people, just don't have what it takes to manage well. We decided to call them Impostor Leaders, because they are attempting to fool us, and often themselves too, that they can lead.

"These managers add less value to organizations than they might do because they cannot engage effectively with others and as a consequence are generally underachievers in terms of the results they generate. The causes of their underperformance are many and varied, but largely stem from their own personal shortcomings which may include: aloofness, insecurity, self-consciousness or even downright laziness.

"We felt that there were two types of Impostor Leaders most frequently encountered: 'Damp Squibs' and 'Dark Clouds'.

"Let's deal with the Damp Squibs first, shall we?" he said.

He then went on to explain that squibs are small detonating devices that resemble miniature sticks of dynamite. In the past, they had a number of applications in mining and military fields; today they are more frequently used for creating special effects for movies. Given that they contain a powder-based explosive, keeping them dry is critical; hence a damp squib is one that fails to explode because it is wet.

"Damp Squib managers constantly fail to ignite," he said. "Actually, it could be said that they have a tendency to implode. They have neither the capacity to fully engage their people nor to achieve anything but an acceptable level of results. We, as a team, have come across a fair few of these leaders in our time and they are often slightly introverted individuals who lack the emotional intelligence needed to really connect with others. They fail to truly understand where other people are coming from.

"Although to be fair to them," he emphasized, "they are not necessarily negative-minded characters, and can often be reasonably upbeat, but when you watch their attempts to interrelate with others, it always feels a bit awkward and forced. For sure, Damp Squibs can be quite intelligent yet they usually lack commonsense and indeed the human touch. Some typical characteristics of these leaders include ..." He lifted back the cover of the flipchart to reveal the following pre-prepared points:

- Insecure characters
- Over-rely on high levels of direction and control
- Micro-manage their people
- Highly cautious
- Often passive-aggressive in nature
- Secretive and like to operate in the shadows
- Slow to make decisions
- Reactive not proactive

Having worked through those points, he then went on to say that Damp Squibs do have the ability, however, to sustain productivity at a level that keeps them in a job; but there is always untapped potential amongst the employees who work for them.

"The collective impact of their bland, controlling nature and general tendency to have their finger in every pie is that certain employees find Damp Squibs simply impossible to work under for very long. In fact, some in our group had seen at first-hand how ambitious individuals with lots of enthusiasm and initiative quickly grew tired of the reactive, pedantic approach adopted by these managers. They felt smothered by the lack of empowerment or autonomy that defined life under them and the need to constantly deal with a 'leader' who craved approval but did not know how, or lacked what was required, to earn it.

"Now, let's move on to the second type of Impostor Leader that we called Dark Clouds.

"These leaders possess many of the same personal failings as Damp Squibs and they too suffer from a general inability to engage employees or to achieve high performance. What particularly differentiates these managers, though, is that they are extremely negative-minded characters who do as little as they can get away with.

"You might think that anyone with all these deficiencies would be quickly found out and, in commercial enterprises, they tend not to survive for too long today. However, one of our group members works in public administration and she says they thrive there, where she has seen a fair few Dark Clouds hanging around."

Mike emphasized that Dark Clouds really couldn't be considered leaders in any true sense of the word and, in fact, they were often shirkers who more or less abdicated the leadership role; their employees certainly seem to feel a strong sense of alienation from them. These managers usually got to their positions not out of any suitability to lead, but more likely because they were simply next in line – that is why they were more frequently found in the public sector.

"To wrap up then," he continued, "working for both kinds of Impostor Leader, we feel, is somewhat akin to having cold water poured over you on a daily basis and the work environment they create is best described as controlling. They can significantly reduce organizational performance, or at the very least, there is always a lot of scope for increased productivity amongst the people working for them.

"Thank you for listening."

Professor de Vreys was again impressed by the quality of the group's work although he did feel that calling these leaders Impostors was somewhat harsh; yet when he opened the debate to the floor, there was general agreement that it was an ideal label for them: fakes pure and simple is what they are.

Finally, the Professor called on the last group who were exploring the Nasty Leaders they had met to outline their findings.

At this, a serious-minded but pleasant woman named Heather stepped forward. As is often the case in the competitive world of executive development each group was seeking to outdo the previous in terms of quirky introductions.

"Trouble is probably a happy little pooch today," she began, "or at least fairly contented one might presume. Not perhaps as satisfied now as before, but in reasonably high spirits all the same; everything worked out well in the end despite all the commotion."

There was a general chuckle around the hall. She had definitely won the prize for off-beat openings.

She went on to say that 'Trouble' was in fact the much loved white Maltese terrier belonging to Leona Helmsley, the deceased billionaire hotelier, that had been bequeathed $12 million in Helmsley's will; more money, in fact, than Ms Helmsley initially left to her brother or indeed to any of her relatives for that matter. Then poor old Trouble had to face a fair bit of trouble of her own.

Heather explained how the pooch started receiving anonymous death threats, or more accurately her keeper got them on her behalf. Apparently, about 20 to 30 in all were received. Things got even worse for the little terrier, as she later lost $10 million of the loot in a court settlement.

"Still," said Heather with a sigh and a smile, "it is fair to assume that there are ample funds left to provide for a happy canine retirement. Trouble certainly does give entirely new meaning to living a dog's life, I think you will agree.

"Being Mrs. Helmsley's dog clearly had its significant rewards," she continued, "but being her employee, it would appear, did not. For sure Trouble seemed to get the better deal from Leona, if her nickname of 'The Queen of Mean' was anything to go by. Stories of her alleged abusive treatment of employees are legendary; she was not the kind of boss you would like to work for by all accounts.

"Oh yes, leadership does indeed have a darkest side," said Heather. "Hidden away in an upstairs room are to be found what our group called 'Toxic Leaders'. These leaders are a dangerous bunch as far as we're concerned and, as a result, deserve a lot of attention. They can, and do, achieve results within the organization but it is in how they do so that creates the problems.

"The behaviors we have seen in these leaders also are naturally varied but we felt as a group that they reflect the worst of those seen in the school playground, except that they carry these juvenile behaviors into adult life. In them can be found a range of destructive conduct including: petty jealousy, sycophantism, bravado, bullying and downright childishness to name but a few. Again, we felt there were two sub-types of Toxic Leaders: 'Egotists' and 'Bullies.'

"Let me start with the Egotists," she said.

"Salvador Dali once proclaimed that 'each morning when I awake, I experience again a supreme pleasure – that of being Salvador Dali.' He certainly didn't suffer from insecurity, but at least his talent as an artist was in direct proportion to his ego.

"Egotists are the Salvador Dalis of organizational life, sharing as they do his aura of grandiosity and believing themselves to be enormously talented individuals. Unfortunately, unlike the great artist – our group agreed – there is usually a gaping hole between their sense of self-worth and reality.

"Despite their outward displays of cockiness, we found that the Egotists we had encountered actually were quite insecure managers, although they would certainly never admit to it. Some of their characteristics include ..." She too revealed a pre-prepared flipchart:

- Arrogant not charismatic
- Often intelligent but never as clever as they think they are
- Driven by self-interest
- Deceitful

- Totally self-centered
- Calculating and manipulative by nature
- Frequently use false charm
- Strongly opinionated

"Egotists are usually not overtly aggressive individuals, however," continued Heather. "They have the ability to maintain a degree of self-control, so they are often very subtle in how they apply their aggression, but they are fairly nasty characters all the same. We were in full agreement that working for Egotists is frustrating and demoralizing for most employees because they realize that they are of secondary concern to these managers. They come to understand that these managers are shallow, superficial individuals who care only about themselves.

"This leads me to our second category of Toxic Leader, the Bullies ... now, let me tell you a thing or two about Bullies," she said, in a manner that made it clear she had dealings with one in the past. This was going to be personal.

"These are the worst kind of bad boss. In our experience, they can be bitter, angry and even unstable characters who suffer from many of the same failings seen in Egotists. But they are largely differentiated from them because they seek to dominate others through their overtly threatening behaviors. Often mildly, if not severely paranoid, Bullies are openly aggressive individuals who lack self-control and as a result have a tendency to explode with rage.

"Generally we agreed as a group, Bullies view work life as a constant battle, one which must be won at all costs and they seem to enjoy inflicting pain on others. Sometimes, it appears that they build themselves up by having someone else to knock down. These leaders survive, and in a few cases thrive, in organizations because they drive performance through fear and intimidation," she said, getting increasingly agitated.

"The arrogant and abrasive nature of Bullies makes them appear confident but, we think that in reality a lot of them, like the Egotists, are insecure individuals who mask that insecurity by trying to show how tough they are. They are often cowards too and when really confronted by someone they can back down but will hold a grudge against that person indefinitely. Unfortunately a lot of people are afraid of Bullies, so they are rarely ..."

For a moment, it was clear that discussing the issue of bullying was bringing back some painful memories for Heather. She took a deep breath and, following encouragement from her fellow team members, picked up where she left off.

"Ehm, rarely challenged is what I wanted to say ... working for Bullies is never a pleasant experience, even when not the target of their abuse. If directly in their sights, individuals can experience severe emotional consequences just like the tormented child in the playground. Even if not in the firing line, Bullies create a stressful environment for everyone and fear of failure drives performance as opposed to any desire to excel.

"I could go on all night about them," she said "but I can see all the tired faces. You get the point anyway, Toxic leaders are a nasty breed but they do exist, and more so than most of us would like.

"Phew, I'm glad that's over, thanks for listening," she said smiling to the watching faces who had long since taken her to their hearts.

At that Professor de Vreys took centre stage once more and again thanked the group for their work and effort. He too could tell that everyone was fading fast, so he got straight to his closing remarks.

"People are not mass-produced goods and they cannot be pigeonholed or slotted into neat little categories just because we would like them to. Each of us is unique, so no two people will, or indeed should, think and act alike all the time. This principle is just as applicable when it comes to leaders.

"Individuality aside, though, what leaders do and how they do it, in my experience, can be far more uniform and predictable than they might like to think, particularly when judged over a sustained period. It is possible, as you have just proven, to start distinguishing leader performance by how well they consistently – and that word is crucial here – combine the leadership and management roles. Of course, each of us can show a range of positive and negative behaviors from time to time – we can all be good, bad and even nasty on occasion. That said, our true behavior patterns ultimately shine through over the longer term.

"Genuine Leaders, as you called them, outshine others in large part because they balance the engage-achieve relationship most of the time. Less effective managers, or the Impostors, as Group B labeled them, fall down on both the engage and achieve side of the equation. They may not always 'fail' as such because outright failure would not be tolerated in most organizations, but they certainly do underperform.

"Finally, the nasty bunch, the Toxic Leaders, as you crowned them, may well achieve results – and that is often what saves them – but they fail to engage people and, as a result, have to drive performance through fear and intimidation, overt or otherwise.

"Clearly it should be obvious to you as to which leader type you should strive to be.

"This has been a most interesting and productive evening," he said, preparing to bring the class to a close. "Two things I would like you to do over the coming week. One is to watch out for the different leader-types as you go about your business in the days ahead. The second is that I would like you to decide which category of leader you currently believe you are and then be prepared to stand up at the next session and tell us why you think you deserve that particular label.

"Thank you and have a nice week," he ended, with a wry smile.

The winner is the chef who takes the same ingredients as everyone else and produces the best results.

Edward de Bono

THE RIGHT STUFF

You get nothing in life if you don't push yourself.

Sounds like a bit of a cliché and it undoubtedly is. Still the man leaning against the lamp post to stretch out his calf muscles actually lives by that creed these days. Although originally his dad's words he genuinely believes in them now, unlike when he was younger and just said he did because ... well, because saying the expected thing at home was just easier. It prevented any arguments from breaking out and there were more than enough of those already without adding fuel to the fire. Obediently repeating any and all mantras made for a bit of peace and quiet, if only temporarily.

Truth is, the guy reaching for his toes used to hate all that 'go get 'em' stuff his dad spouted. It was just some bogus twaddle peddled by ex-Marines, or so he thought at the time. But that had changed over the years. Why? Well, for one, he had simply grown up and stopped acting like a complete knucklehead. But he probably started to really believe in the power of self-motivation once he quit smoking pot after he left college; yeah, pushing himself became a whole lot easier then.

Now every weekday morning at around 6.30 or so, come hail, rain or shine, Mike Douglas can be seen exiting his block and stepping out onto Rector Place in the south of the city to begin the same stretching regime each day.

He isn't a complete fitness fanatic, mind you, unlike many of the health freaks in the neighborhood with their wheatgrass smoothies and the like; he is still well-known for letting his hair down every now and again. But he gets a real buzz out of jogging, particularly first thing. It gives him time to think, sets him up for the day ahead and helps him to stay sharp. As his father had said when he was growing up – over and over and over again – a healthy body made for a healthy mind. Turns out he was actually right.

On this day, a cloudy early spring morning, Mike planned to turn left onto South End Avenue and jog across to the Esplanade, then continue south alongside the Hudson River into Battery Park where he would be met, if it wasn't too foggy out on the water, with spectacular views of the Statue of Liberty and Ellis Island. From there, he would do an about-turn, head for the Irish Hunger Memorial at Vesey Street before turning for home.

The circuit he visualized in his mind as he warmed up wasn't all that demanding but it would be enough to get the heart pumping. And his target was to take a full minute off the previous day's time. A big ask.

As he set off in the patchy sunshine, his thoughts turned not to the day ahead but beyond it to the next session of his development program due to take place that evening at CNYU. He had spent all week thinking about what type of leader he was. Well, no, this was not entirely accurate for he hadn't actually spent the time focusing on that aspect of the task they had been set. In truth, he was pretty clear where he sat on the spectrum from nasty to good leaders. Without any trace of arrogance, and those who knew him would testify that he was not in any way afflicted by it, he positioned himself towards the Genuine Leader end of the scale.

For sure he recognized that he was far from a polished diamond with lots still to learn, but as he approached his 38th birthday, he also knew that the feedback received about his leadership over the years had consistently been positive.

Okay the tag 'Genuine Leader' had never actually featured, that was just how one of the groups on the program had labeled excellent leaders the previous week. But after graduating – not with flying colors it must be said – and probably more importantly, after he got his act together, he had regularly been singled out for praise in his career to date for his ability to lead, in different companies and at different levels. Even the most recent evaluation in his current position – SVP, Corporate Strategy & Business Development – had rated his overall talents as a manager highly, with particular merit attached to his capacity to engage and inspire others.

So he hadn't spent the week trying to position himself on the leadership spectrum, instead he was more focused on the second part of the assignment: how best to describe what he believed underpinned and contributed to that positioning.

And picking up the pace, he knew that it was this element of the assignment that would be of most interest to Professor de Vreys, or so it appeared, if his wry smile at the end of the previous week's session was anything to go by. Mike knew that the Professor was no fool, far from it, and he would be expecting everyone in the class to place themselves at the good leader end of the scale. Duh, that was pretty obvious.

But could they explain why they believed themselves to be so? That was the real answer the Professor was likely seeking.

On the one hand Mike knew he could, as some of his classmates had already indicated they were likely to do, just offer up some *blah-blah* answers about his engaging personality, ability to empathize or high levels of assertiveness – all of which were valid in his case. But the days of taking the easy route were long gone for him. Whereas some of those attending the program seemed to consider this particular task as being too 'junior' for people at their level, Mike took the opposite view. He felt it was actually quite incisive in terms of getting them to really think about what drove their success as managers. After all if they really understood those drivers then they could better focus their personal development efforts in future.

Mike therefore wanted to come up with something more becoming of an executive development program: a framework, perhaps, or an integrated structure – but nothing too nerdy – that would bring together all the various components he felt contributed to his success as a leader. He considered this program to be an important stepping-stone to the remainder of his career and he wanted to shine on it, not just do the bare minimum or come up with the easy solutions.

What's more, he also understood that any positive feedback regarding his overall performance on the course that might make its way back to his boss *via* the Professor could only but help his chances of gaining a place on the firm's Operating Committee when the decision was made later in the year. And that was his priority short-term goal.

So for a variety of reasons, it was worth any and all the effort he put into the program and specifically into that week's project.

As he turned for the home stretch, he had to negotiate his way past some sidewalk improvement works taking place – the 'Keep Right' sign sending him totally off his intended path; knocking that minute off was going to be even harder as a result. When he found his way back to his normal route after the detour, for some reason he was suddenly reminded of a book he had read a long time back. It began to play on his mind.

A nagging feeling grew within him that there might be something, an idea, or a concept within it that could give him a tool to work with as he attempted to describe what he believed were the foundations of his leadership effectiveness. The book he was thinking about was *The Right Stuff*, by Tom Wolfe, a classic story that painted a vivid picture of the American military pilots who had helped to pioneer the NASA Space Program and described how the seven Mercury astronauts were selected and later trained.

Although the book was largely about the heroism of these men it particularly focused on who they were as people and how they lived by an unspoken set of standards and assumptions that set them apart from lesser mortals. It was this aspect of the story – what it was that made those guys special – that was still bouncing around his head as he buzzed himself back into his building.

He hadn't bettered the previous day's time but there was always tomorrow. Anyway he was off on a different mission.

Having showered and readied himself for work, Mike had found the book once more, after a fair bit of drawer-tossing. Sitting in his kitchen, coffee cup in hand, he flicked through the well-worn pages until he came to the one he was looking for. It was where Wolfe described what set those astronauts apart:

As to just what this ineffable quality was ... well, it obviously involved bravery. But it was not bravery in the simple sense of being willing to risk your life ... any fool could do that ... No, the idea ... seemed to be that a man should have the ability to go up in a hurtling piece of machinery and put his hide on the line and then have the moxie, the reflexes, the experience, the coolness, to pull back

*in the last yawning moment – and then to go up again the next day,
and the next day, and every next day ... There was ... a seemingly
infinite series of tests. ... a dizzy progression of steps and ledges, a
ziggurat, a pyramid extraordinarily high and steep; and the idea
was to prove at every foot of the way up that pyramid that you were
one of the elected and anointed ones who had the right stuff and
could move higher and higher and even – ultimately, God willing,
one day – that you might be able to join that special few at the very
top, that elite who had the capacity to bring tears to men's eyes, the
very Brotherhood of the Right Stuff itself.*

It was the very idea of 'the right stuff' which had been playing on
his mind, that's what the niggling feeling had been about.

Sure he understood that while this particular description worked
well for astronauts, it was clearly not all that relevant to managers;
yet he felt that successful leaders too needed something special and
having some form of *the right stuff* was essential in any leadership
context.

That said, he knew that it was hardly revolutionary to promote
the idea that people needed certain traits and skills to manage
effectively but as he headed out the door, he was happy that he now
had an idea to work with. A solid foundation: something to be built
upon.

Taking the subway from Rector Street to 66th and Lincoln
Center he was lost in his own world, oblivious to the throng
of people around him. Why is it, he wondered, that some
individuals fail the leadership challenge to the extent that they
create a deep-seated resentment in those around them, whereas
others can manage in such a way as to generate great loyalty from
their employees to the point where it can, on occasion, verge on a
form of devotion? What is it that sets them apart?

He felt he had some of whatever 'it' was but how to capture and
explain those features in simple but meaningful terms was the
challenge.

For all that he had read and heard on the subject of leadership over the years, too often, or so it seemed to him, the question of why some managers outshine others was answered in the narrow context of what they 'do.' Do more of the right things more of the time, went the argument, and a leader's performance will improve. Certainly, he knew that what any manager did was a key determinant of their success because ultimately they were judged by their actions, or more precisely, the outcomes that arose from them.

But as he swayed from side-to-side in perfect harmony with the carriage, he felt that this over-emphasis on the 'doing' bit somehow missed a fundamental point.

"Before I do anything, I am someone," he said to himself, "and who I am and how I think sets the tone for what I do and it directly influences how well I am able to do it." From his experience, and indeed from watching and talking to other more senior executives, he felt that the inner-self was a major driver of success as a leader, and in life generally.

Unfortunately, he thought, the contribution of the inner-self to management success, whilst not completely ignored, seemed to be downplayed. Perhaps this was due to the fact that focusing on what makes you tick can seem like a fuzzy topic, or akin to navel-gazing – a bit too Oprah to be of any real value in the cut-throat world of business. One thing was most definitely clear in his mind: he did not want to come across that evening as wishy-washy, or in some way wooly by following this train of thought.

But he really did believe that achievement in any field of human activity, including management, actually started with what's inside; it did not, he was convinced, simply result from the skills someone had or could develop from what they knew or could learn. After all something drove him to pick his ass up off the couch all those years ago and stop goofing his way through life.

So despite his concerns about communicating his ideas in a meaningful way to the Professor and his classmates, he felt that any description of his success to date as a leader could not ignore who he was and how he thought as crucial foundations of his capacity to lead.

When he hit street level, he decided to give his father a call to see if he was around for lunch. His dad, a successful manager in his own right, always had some valuable insights to offer on any work-related matter. Although for many years, particularly as a teenager, Mike had sneered at most of what his father believed and said, the relationship had first softened, then strengthened over the years. He now knew that the Old Man was the best person to bounce some of his ideas off; if they didn't stack up in terms of credibility, he wouldn't be long putting Mike straight.

Thankfully his father was free and they arranged to meet at 1pm at a restaurant called The Madison on West 64th Street, not far from the office.

Slipping the cell phone back into his breast pocket and pulling his collar up slightly against the light rain he marched along in sync with the early riser crowd, still focused on how he might tailor his message that evening.

He felt a tap on the shoulder.

"Morning, Mike, how are you today? In another world by the look of it."

He turned to greet his CEO.

"I'm great, thanks," he answered, while slowing to match the boss's stride.

As they walked and talked, the subject of his participation on the CNYU Program naturally arose. Mike explained the current focus of the leadership module and outlined what he was working on in terms of the right stuff concept, adding honestly how he was struggling to find the best way to communicate that message.

When they entered the building his CEO, not surprisingly given his style, suggested they grab a quick coffee together in the cafeteria. "I'm not going to provide you with the answer, Mike," he stressed with a smile, "but, if at all possible, I will be happy to steer you in the right direction."

Standing in a quiet corner of the café area – and after a somewhat unwanted interruption from a colleague who came over to greet the boss – Mike made the case that, in his opinion, all too frequently leadership potential was too narrowly focused on the skills part, but he was convinced that how leaders think and who they are on the inside was equally, if not far more, important. His big fear, though, was he might sound like a bit of a hippy if he focused too much on that aspect of a manager's make-up.

His boss listened intently to his concerns – offering no conclusions either way – other than to tell Mike to look out for a study called *Ten Fatal Flaws that Derail Leaders*, by two guys named Jack Zenger and Joseph Folkman. This work, he suggested, might help him to sort out his thinking on the issue. And with that recommendation his CEO was off. He had a hectic day ahead.

Later Mike sat at his desk and searched online for the study. He quickly found a synopsis in the *Harvard Business Review* and, as he read through the article, a particular extract caught his eye.

He printed it off:

To find out why leaders fail, we scrutinized results from two studies: In one, we collected 360-degree feedback data on more than 450 Fortune 500 executives and then teased out the common characteristics of the 31 who were fired over the next three years. In the second, we analyzed 360-degree feedback data from more than 11,000 leaders and identified the 10% who were considered least effective. We then compared the ineffective leaders with the fired leaders to come up with the 10 most common leadership shortcomings. Every bad leader had at least one, and most had several. Bad leaders:

Lack energy and enthusiasm. *They see new initiatives as a burden, rarely volunteer, and fear being overwhelmed. One such leader was described as having the ability to 'suck all the energy out of any room.'*

Accept their own mediocre performance. *They overstate the difficulty of reaching targets so that they look good when they achieve them. They live by the mantra 'under-promise and over-deliver'.*

Lack clear vision and direction. *They believe their only job is to execute. Like a hiker who sticks close to the trail, they're fine until they come to a fork.*

Have poor judgment. They make decisions that colleagues and subordinates consider to be not in the organization's best interests.

Don't collaborate. They avoid peers, act independently, and view other leaders as competitors. As a result, they are set adrift by the very people whose insights and support they need.

Don't walk the talk. They set standards of behavior or expectations of performance and then violate them. They're perceived as lacking integrity.

Resist new ideas. They reject suggestions from subordinates and peers. Good ideas aren't implemented, and the organization gets stuck.

Don't learn from mistakes. They may make no more mistakes than their peers, but they fail to use setbacks as opportunities for improvement, hiding their errors and brooding about them instead.

Lack interpersonal skills. They make sins of both commission (they're abrasive and bullying) and omission (they're aloof, unavailable, and reluctant to praise).

Fail to develop others. They focus on themselves to the exclusion of developing subordinates, causing individuals and teams to disengage.

Mike could see quickly that most of the flaws found in the surveyed leaders related as much to who they were as people as they did to the talents or skills they may or may not have possessed. This confirmed to him that skills and knowledge alone, whilst obviously essential, were of little use if a manager did not have certain personal characteristics and a way of thinking that underpins positive leadership. He was more convinced than ever that the best leaders are something before they actually do anything.

It is, he thought, who I am, as much as what I do that has impacted on my ability to become an effective leader.

For the rest of the morning Mike had little time to focus on anything but pressing matters at hand and it was only as he strolled over to meet his father for lunch that the right stuff concept came floating back into his mind. He was quite looking forward to meeting his dad as it had been more than a few months since they had hooked up; he felt bad, as usual, about having left it so long.

His father, a successful CEO for many years, had retired a couple of months previously; well, retired in name only, it had to be said, because as far as Mike knew he was busier than ever what with the consulting, advising, sitting on various boards and God knows what else. Entering the restaurant he quickly caught a glimpse of his dad through the crowd. Unsurprisingly he was already deep in conversation with someone he knew.

"Hey, Pop, how's the life of leisure treating you? Boy, it sure is well for some, isn't it? Sitting in restaurants all day chatting to old pals."

His father smiled and introduced the elderly gentleman at the table as a one-time colleague; from the manner and tone of the introduction it was clear to Mike that his dad held this guy in high esteem. After some reflection on days gone by, on the passing of time and on the importance of family, the man made to take his leave. "See you soon, Boss," he signaled to Mike's father as a struggle began to haul creaking bones upright.

Mike's dad rose quickly to his feet and helped his aged friend out of the chair, then walked slowly arm-in-arm with him to a banquette at the back of the room. There, he guided him into a seat, shaking hands with what appeared to be his wife and family, before returning to join Mike.

"So, how are you, son?"

"I'm great thanks."

They chatted generally during lunch, bringing each other up-to-date on life since they had last seen each other, both apologizing for the lapse in contact but neither really being offended by it. They might not have always seen each other as often as they would have liked but they were pretty close nonetheless and the deep antagonism of old had long since disappeared. As they later sipped coffee his father switched to his serious voice.

"Right-so, son, what was it that you wanted to talk to me about?"

Mike jokingly tried to explain that he had simply wished to see his beloved father after such a long time but he got a look that said 'cut-the-bull'. He laughed and then told his dad about the CNYU Program, its current focus on his own leadership capabilities and his proposal to use the right stuff concept as a way of explaining why he felt he had succeeded as a manager to date.

His father listened quietly and when Mike had finished, he replied.

"You know, Mike, I am a big believer that in any walk of life, talent or skills are never the primary differentiators between those who make it and others who don't reach the same heights. I could labor the damn point, but I think nothing highlights this quite as well as an encounter I heard of between John Daly, the talented but wayward golfer, and Tiger Woods, that now-flawed genius.

"Apparently at one tournament Daly was sitting enjoying a beer with friends when Tiger passed the table on his way to the gym. Daly shouted across to Tiger asking him whether he never got tired of exercising and invited him to join them for a drink. Tiger quipped back, 'If I had your talent, I wouldn't need to exercise'.

"Just think about that for a moment, son, because there is a helluva lot of learning in those few words if you really think about it. Now, as you well know, I'm no great golfer but I can tell you that Tiger Woods has not achieved all that he has done on the golf course purely because of his high skill levels and scratch handicap. Actually, many in the know would argue that John Daly has at times shown equal flair with a club.

"What Daly seemed to lack, though, was the drive, determination and discipline that made Tiger such a special player, which is best captured in his own words that, as far as I remember, went something like this: 'I love to play golf, and that's my arena. And you can characterize it and describe it however you want, but I have a love and a passion for getting that ball in the hole and beating those guys.'

"Well," continued his dad smiling, "we now know that Tiger had other off-course passions as well, but you cannot ignore the fact that he had that little bit extra required to make it as a top golfer for a sustained period. John Daly, on the other hand, came up a bit short in that regard most of the time. Being consistently the best at anything requires more than just talent or skill and this applies not only in golfing circles but in all areas of life, and, believe you me, that includes management.

"For sure Tiger's personal reputation has taken a battering in recent times and, whatever the rights and wrongs of it all, his recent woes simply prove to me that the man is human. By the way it also demonstrates that the inner-self can lead us in the wrong direction as well as the right one. In the end it will be in how he continues to pick up the pieces in the years ahead that the true measure of the man will emerge.

"Just like how you turned things around all those years ago, son," he said, as he patted Mike on the shoulder. "Your mother would be very proud at how you've turned out. Actually we should probably talk at some stage about the future, son, seeing as it is just the two of us now ..."

His father had never acknowledged the changes Mike had made in his life, and he rarely mentioned his mother since her death, nor did he ever do 'talks' about the future, so there was an awkward silence, as there can only ever be between a father and son when neither knows what to say next. Then his dad chose the safe option.

"Despite all the damage done to Tiger's image what he has achieved on the golf course will stand the test of time and how he did so still presents positive lessons that can be applied in a management context: first, that talent on its own is never a guarantee of success but also that we all have angels and demons within us that contribute to how we act and behave."

As ever his father had cut through the haze and with a very straightforward example, he had assured Mike that he was on track with his thinking. The emotional stuff, well, best not to dwell on all that, Mike thought.

"Do you think people might view what I am saying about the right stuff as being too simple, Dad?" he asked finally, as they stood to leave.

"It is undoubtedly simple, son, but it's far from simplistic."

At that, they said their goodbyes, vowing, as they always did, not to let so much time pass before their next get-together.

"By the way, son," his father shouted after him, "I think there's a girl named Jane Griffiths on that program of yours. She's one of the young managers from my old firm. Give her my best regards when next you see her."

L ater that evening Professor de Vreys called Mike to the front of the lecture hall for his turn to explain where he stood as a leader, and more importantly, to describe what it was that had helped him to achieve that positioning on the leadership spectrum. Mike greeted his classmates and then called up on screen the one slide he had prepared for his talk.

The Right Stuff

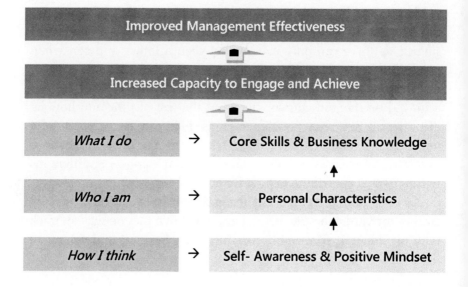

He began his presentation with a quote from Abraham Maslow, the renowned psychologist:

> *Whereas the average individuals often have not the slightest idea of what they are, of what they want, of what their own opinions are, self-actualizing individuals have superior awareness of their own impulses, desires, opinions, and subjective reactions in general.*

"If you were sending someone to the moon you would probably want them to have something special about them," he continued as he broke into his stride ...

Everyone thinks of changing the world, but no one thinks of changing himself.

Leo Tolstoy

OBLIVIOUS

"Elephants are self-aware. At least, they are, based on the findings of research conducted at Bronx Zoo with Asian elephants ..."

Steve Howley turned up the volume on his radio. He liked to stay abreast of developments in any field; tidbits of information usually came in handy at some point, particularly if you knew how to use them. After all a little knowledge could be made to go a long way.

He listened intently as the reporter explained how, according to a recent study, researchers using specially-designed mirrors had proven that elephants can recognize their own reflections, something until then it was believed that only humans, apes and to some extent dolphins could do. One of the researchers – a Dr. Someone-or-other – then described how surprised they had been at the speed with which the elephants came to terms with their own image and began interacting with the mirror; they did not appear to mistake their reflections for strangers and try to greet them, as the researchers had suspected they might do.

Steve remained enthralled as the Doc went on to explain that this self-awareness seemingly contributes to the social complexity seen in elephant herds, and could be linked to the empathy and concern for others in the group that they have been known to display. "Even now," he ended, "we know only a fraction about their true capacity for self-awareness ..."

Well thank you for that great insight. Now back to you in the studio.

"Always knew they were intriguing creatures," Steve mumbled to himself as he turned into the underground car park on West 66th Street. Taking a left off the ramp towards the entrance lobby, he slotted his top-of-the-range Lexus into one of the empty spaces closest to the main elevator – the best spots were usually free at that hour. It was exactly 7am.

As ever he noted the time on the small scratch-pad mounted on the dashboard. He also noticed that the boss's car was not yet to be seen, although he knew that the CEO didn't always drive in; still, he felt a strong sense of satisfaction that, once again, he had likely arrived before him. Such things mattered, he assured himself, for they showed true commitment and dedication. It was these seemingly innocuous details that could swing the vote in his favor come decision-time and, for a man on the move such as himself, there was always a decision-time of some sort or other on the horizon.

Climbing out of his seat he stood for a moment beside the car and, catching his reflection in the side window, he flicked some stray hair back into place, fixed his collar, straightened his tie and tweaked his cufflinks. He then opened the back door to retrieve his Regent Stripe jacket. Carefully he put it on and brushed himself down with the double-sided-soft-bristle he always kept in the glove compartment. Looks mattered after all.

He was ready for the day ahead.

Since joining the company as SVP, Product Development a number of years earlier Steve had set himself some challenging goals, the primary one being to gain a seat upon the Operating Committee, or the OC as he liked to call it. This was now, he recognized as he took the elevator to the 15th floor, a target well within reach because there was an incumbent member due to retire at the end of the current year. Grabbing that vacancy was weighing heavily on his mind of late. *Heading towards an obsession, if you were to ask his wife.*

As he watched each floor indicator light brighten then fade during the ascent, Steve knew that securing the much sought-after position on the six-strong body required his continued mastery of 'The Game', as he had christened it, or in other words he had to focus relentlessly on three areas.

First up, of course, he had to deliver on the targets established for the Product Development Division – without producing the required outcomes in that area, any thoughts of future progression were clearly immaterial. To do that he needed his team to deliver for him, and this in turn meant maintaining his unparalleled performance as a leader to ensure they were continuously productive to the nth degree. Finally, he was not naïve and realized that there were a number of his colleagues chasing the same end, so staying ahead of the competition was therefore vital.

A *ting* sounded and the doors opened. *Seconds Out, Round One,* he thought to himself as he stepped out onto the corridor.

Steve marched past the still dark offices and his thoughts turned once more to The Game, as they frequently did. He was in it FTW, as the guys at the club were fond of saying – or 'for the win' to the uninitiated. To that end, apart from his undoubted flair in his chosen field – his talent for product development was widely acknowledged – it was, he believed, his innate ability to read others, to stay one step ahead of them, that gave him a real edge over his rivals; and not just in the race for the seat on the OC either, but in the wider game itself. As he had learned from reading Sun Tzu in *The Art of War* 'to know your enemy, you must become your enemy.'

He was a true general.

On the one hand this ability to get inside the heads of others meant that he knew how to court favor with his superiors; and, after all, no game was ever won without pleasing those who controlled it. Over the years he had figured out what made each one of those top brass tick so he could first anticipate – yes, it was always vital to anticipate – and then respond to their needs, thereby putting himself in their good books. Make sure to give them what they wanted, that was the key.

And even when he needed something from them, his talent for mind games meant he could do so in a way that made them feel that they were actually the driving force behind what were, in truth, his ideas. He knew how to give them the 'invisible steering wheel', as he liked to describe it, whereby he subtly sowed seeds in their minds and they headed in the direction he wanted them to go.

Flicking on the lights in his office he sat at his desk and then switched on his computer. As the screen sputtered to life he continued to think about how he stood apart in The Game.

When it came to his employees he could read them like a book too and he knew that his overall approach to management was another area where he excelled.

He had a simple leadership philosophy.

As most people liked to be shown the way or craved direction – and due to the fact that the buck ultimately stopped with him – he believed it was vital that any decisions taken, or actions implemented, within the Division had to have his fingerprints all over them. Nothing of importance – and ultimately everything was important to some degree when set in the context of the bigger picture – could happen on his patch without his approval. He kept a tight hold of the reins.

In doing so he exercised high levels of control over his employees generally, but particularly his direct-report managers, not in an aggressive manner for that would probably have been counterproductive, but nonetheless he needed to pull all the strings. Although he had inherited, for the most part, an intelligent and hard working team, be that as it may, he felt they did not truly understand the nuances of corporate life or the complexities of the business environment to the extent that he did. Hence the necessity for continuous direction from him.

Certainly he had never heard any complaints from his people about this approach. But why would they have any problems with it? After all weren't they benefitting from his vast wisdom and experience?

Okay it was true that a number of senior managers in the Division had left since the start of his tenure but this was only to be expected, as some people were simply unable to cope with the higher performance expectations he held in comparison to those of his predecessor. If you can't stand the heat and all that.

Prompted by the screen command he entered his password and hit the return key.

Although he constantly took the lead so that his employees could follow, it was not the case, however, that there was no room for consultation with his key people. That, of course, would have looked bad in this day and age. But he believed that individual involvement should be focused where it could add greatest value.

So his senior team could make a real contribution in determining implementation plans, once the overall direction had been set by him. He defined the concepts for all new products and they brought his vision to life. This approach, he felt, they warmly embraced because his proactive style of leadership removed the stress associated with strategic decision-making.

What's more, his style not only ensured that he was advancing his own goals, but in the process, he was also helping to develop certain individuals within the Division by providing them with an insight, a master-class even, into how effective management worked in practice. This was clearly a win-win situation for everyone concerned.

As he waited for the computer to boot he scanned through the appointments list that his assistant had left on his desk the evening before.

Another of his unique selling points came to mind.

He was the king when it came to managing execution. Of that there was no doubt. Yes, he was someone who made things happen. The results for his Division proved it.

And he was proud of the fact that he always allowed his people complete autonomy of action during the implementation phase. His role, another vital leadership function he believed, was to get out of the way and let them do their thing. Instead he supported their efforts by closely monitoring their progress, offering continuous advice and assistance, questioning their rationale at every step, showing them how to improve their ideas, recommending a change in direction if necessary, and generally guiding them to ensure that the outcomes were as he expected.

He was always there to help, every single hour of every single day.

Indeed over recent years, he had noticed how his senior managers had increasingly preferred to wait for that help rather than take the initiative, which further reinforced his belief that they appreciated, not to say needed, his ongoing input. This willingness to support his people was another area in which he felt he excelled.

Dah-Dah came the sound as his computer announced its readiness but he was in a daze. He stared blankly at the screen.

Despite his many undoubted strengths as a manager he was still only too well aware that he needed to keep a close eye on those peers whom he considered to be direct competitors in The Game. It was an ongoing struggle.

These individuals, he knew, would gladly throw him to the lions given half a chance – and due to the fact that one or two had already shown their resentment of him by criticizing aspects of his performance, this only further confirmed the need to monitor their actions closely, or more importantly, to stay attuned to the shifting alliances amongst the executive management team in order to ensure that he wasn't sidelined or marginalized in any way.

The chatter of others passing his door brought him back from the battlefield. He pulled his chair closer to the desk, shifted focus and got down to work.

Steve's daily routine when in the office tended to follow a similar pattern. He liked structure. It was, he felt, a sign of a disciplined mind. His first action was always to scan for any Google Alerts indicating that his name had featured somewhere in the media the previous day. Where something was noted, he circulated the link to top people within the company. He was sure they would be eager to know.

This issue of visibility, both within the organization and across the wider industry, was another critical component of The Game. He knew how important it was that his achievements were subtly communicated, particularly to the CEO; on top of that it was essential that he always put his best foot forward when the opportunity arose for direct interaction with the C-Suite crowd.

To that end he not only needed to be an expert in his own functional area but also to stay tuned to developments in other business activities so that he could engage effectively during management meetings or at other events. He was glad that, on many occasions, he had been in a position to offer his advice and expertise on matters that did not directly concern him.

His next early task was usually to check his inbox. In general Steve was a big fan of email because he truly believed it to be the best mode of internal and external communication in a fast-paced world: but only when it was used properly, of course. For sure when he had taken over the Division, there had been far too much sloppiness tolerated by his predecessor when it came to emails, so he had created a set of rules for his team that clearly specified how to structure and write emails of various types, including the correct usage of the BCC and CC alternatives which, in his opinion, had been widely misused.

Since the sending of that five-page memo, he had noticed a distinct improvement in the quality of emails circulating within the team. It was outcomes such as this that confirmed to him that written communications far outweighed face-to-face approaches when important issues had to be widely communicated.

Another great advantage of email, he firmly believed, was that it reduced the need for constant meetings which meant dragging everybody away from their desks unnecessarily. Emails were therefore not only a priority communication tool but also helped to raise productivity across the Division.

Perhaps most beneficial of all, emails also provided an enduring record of his instructions, or decisions, so they prevented any confusion arising later as to what his precise wishes had been.

Meetings, of course, could not be avoided entirely and indeed had their limited benefits but when held, they needed to be tightly controlled. Steve participated in far too many meetings within the firm that, to his mind, were unstructured and ineffective, so he made sure this did not happen within his own Division. As a result he chaired all meetings with his senior managers, provided focus and direction for discussions, shared his expertise, challenged wayward thinking, corrected misconceptions, explained hard-to-understand subjects, identified lessons to be learned and generally helped them to arrive at decisions more effectively by offering his views on each and every subject at hand.

Confirmation of his talent for managing meetings frequently was to be found when he allowed opportunities for general discussion during the wrap-up. Since he had taken over there had been a steady and noticeable decline in the points raised at the end of each meeting. Obviously he was covering all their concerns during the discussions so there was little need for further questioning.

The fact that his team also seemed very eager to get back to work after these meetings further confirmed to him, not only how dedicated they were, but also the importance of keeping such distractions to a minimum so they could concentrate on their work.

Having used his early arrival to plan out his day and to circulate any necessary instructions to relevant parties, Steve then left his office and made his way down to the cafeteria. This was another important part of the daily routine. As many employees, including the boss, gathered for a quick coffee each morning, it was essential, he felt, always to make an appearance.

Upon arrival he made sure that he first 'shared experiences', as he called it, with any of the senior executives who may be present. On this particular day it did not go unnoticed that Mike, one of the people he considered as a main rival for the position on the OC, seemed to be having a cozy chat with the boss. Steve made a point of swinging by where they were standing to say hello; a little early morning fishing expedition, if you like.

He knew that Mike had recently been nominated to attend some development program or other, but he saw this not as a threat; rather he had convinced himself it was a positive reflection on him or an affirmation of his talents. He had not been chosen, he believed, simply because there was an understanding at senior levels that he did not need further development to the extent that others did.

However he was slightly annoyed upon seeing them together because, judging by the umbrella at the CEO's side, it appeared as if he had not traveled by car that day and as such would likely have failed to notice Steve's early arrival.

Steve then mingled with those of his managers or employees who were in the area. This was again something he did every day and, when in the building, he also tried to join his team members at other break times or for lunch, if at all possible. Making this effort, he understood, not only showed his concern for them but also provided an ideal opportunity for those present to chat to him about any matter that might be on their minds or important issues that needed input from him.

The fact that they seemed to clam up in his presence was something he found quite endearing, as it was clearly a sign that they felt a little overawed in his presence.

To help his employees overcome this shyness he made a strong effort to engage them at their level because he did not want them to feel awkward around him. As ever he was the first to instigate the conversation which, on this morning, related to the important game that had been played the night before; he had heard details about it on the radio during the drive to work. Whilst he spoke he thought to himself how this ability to chat casually to people on many different subjects was another important skill that helped him to stand out.

He was a VKP, or a Very Knowledgeable Person.

At the close of play Steve – always one of the last to leave – reflected on the day's events as he made the journey home. This particular evening, just as he had left the city, an important feedback point for one of his managers came to mind, as often happened; he notified her immediately by Blackberry, knowing full well that she would be eager to hear about her area for improvement regardless of the hour.

As he drove he once again picked up on his train of thought from earlier in the day: what it was that helped him to tower over others, not only in the race for the spot on the OC, but in The Game itself. Ultimately aside from his recognized flair for product development, his great personal qualities, his ability to read and manage people, his success at execution, his knack for communicating with others at all levels – apart from all of this – he largely attributed his overall success to his strong self-awareness. It pushed him to constantly raise his game so, unlike others, he was improving all the time. This, he was sure, would stand him in good stead over those whose names were likely to appear on any shortlist for the seat on the OC. In fact he could really only see one name emerging victorious.

Thoughts of self-awareness reminded him of something. He vowed to share that interesting tidbit about elephants with his wife over dinner.

How we think shows through in how we act.
Attitudes are mirrors of the mind.
They reflect thinking.

David Joseph Schwartz

MINDSET MATTERS

Karl Anderson sat expressionless in his chair, arms folded and eyes forward. His carefully constructed appearance of calm was betrayed by a soft rhythmic *tap-tap-tapping*; the sound of a treacherous foot as it exposed the inner turmoil.

He came to sit in that room often, yet knew nothing of it. For the past three years, once every six months or so, he was politely ushered through the door to wait in that space, but he could likely tell you little about his surroundings: the certificates on the wall, the magazines fanned neatly across the antique table, the coffee and juice station, none of these things registered.

The impending results were all that mattered.

He had been crestfallen on first hearing the news. It had come to him couched in a well rehearsed sentence but he had heard just one word: Mel-an-oma. The intended comfort offered by accompanying phrases like 'early stage', 'can be fully contained' and 'nothing in the lymph nodes' was lost on him at first. Mel-an-oma was all he had heard, over and over in his head. *Lentigo Maligna Melanoma.*

The surgery went well, Dr. Rodman had assured him, and the biopsy had removed it all. The upside, she told him in her matter-of-fact tone, was that no further treatment was prescribed. The downside was that there were no guarantees as to what the future might hold. She was a doctor after all, not a clairvoyant. Since then, it was simply a case of following her advice, attending for regular check-ups and ultimately, just hoping and praying for the best.

Karl did all of those things.

As he sat and stared he remembered what had happened when he first told his family and friends about the diagnosis. He had watched with an oddly detached amusement the many different reactions to what he had said; some were automatically optimistic, whereas others seemed devastated at what he had told them.

During the testing stage when the full picture was still unknown, he had bounced back quickly from the initial shock and remained upbeat throughout, as he tended to do about most things, and people like his Uncle Bob were the same, refusing to let the negativity take hold. Not everyone took the same view, though: his mother in particular was terribly downbeat until the final results came through. Then again she tended to be fairly pessimistic about most things.

Shifting uncomfortably in the chair he was reminded too of something else that had happened back then. When his own doctor had first broken the news about the need to refer him to a specialist, he had prepared an information pack for Karl to take home with him. It had sat unopened on a shelf in the kitchen for several weeks before he bothered to scan through it; when he did, most of it was just general information about skin cancer. There was, however, one photocopied sheet that had proven far more valuable.

It was an extract from an article in *The New York Times* by Richard A. Friedman, M.D. under the headline, *Yet Another Worry for Those Who Believe the Glass Is Half-Empty* and it referred to a study about how mindset affects recovery rates in patients. Sitting there waiting for Dr. Rodman, he uncrossed his arms, fished out his wallet and removed the neatly-folded piece of paper.

Carefully opening the sheet he read the extract once more to pass the time:

The study, led by Dr. Erik J. Giltay of the Psychiatric Center GGZ Delfland and published in the Archives of General Psychiatry, *followed 941 Dutch subjects, ages 65 to 85, from 1991 to 2001. Subjects were ranked in quartiles as pessimistic or optimistic on the basis of their reactions to statements like "I still have positive expectations concerning my future" and "I often feel that life is full of promise."*

Dr. Giltay and his colleagues found that subjects with the highest level of optimism were 45% less likely than those with the highest level of pessimism to die of all causes during the study. For those in the quartile with the highest optimism score, the death rate was 30.4%; those in the most pessimistic quartile had a death rate of 56.5% ...

Dr. Giltay carefully controlled for baseline risk factors like blood pressure, cholesterol, smoking and alcohol consumption in his study. Even after controlling for these confounding variables, there was still a significant excess of mortality in the pessimists compared with the optimists. And when he factored in the subjects' own perception of their health — optimists, not surprisingly, report feeling better — pessimists still had higher morbidity and mortality.

He folded the paper again and put it away. He thought it pretty clever of his doctor to have given him the article at that difficult stage. As a wallet closed, a door opened. A leg stopped tapping. A heart began to race.

"It's all good news thankfully, Karl," said the specialist as she approached, "nothing of concern this visit. Just keep focused on what we've agreed and see you later in the year as scheduled."

She didn't, as Karl had come to recognize, do long conversations or indulge in any sort of emotional bonding with her patients and, once she had answered his few questions, she shook his hand and left. A bit of a cold sort, he always felt but, hey, that was her way, and seeing as she was reputed to be the best consultant in town, Dr. Helen could be as aloof as she wished.

Although she may have been sparing with her words the enormity of the relief carried within them was hard to describe; an unnoticed weight immediately lifted from his shoulders every time he got the all-clear. "So far, so good," he said aloud, punching his fist in the air – to the bemusement of passersby – as he stepped with a spring out onto 7th Avenue.

From there he always made the short walk to Our Lady of Pompeii Church at the corner of Bleecker and Carmine where he sat for a while in the relative calm and gave thanks for another good result; 6-0 and counting, he thought, as he silently updated his Maker on the score. Upon leaving the church this time, with the rest of the afternoon free, he decided to buy a sandwich and stroll the few blocks to James J. Walker Park to sit in the light sunshine.

E njoying the tuna melt he had bought his thoughts turned to more mundane matters, namely the assignment he had been given as part of the Executive Development Program he was attending at CNYU. At the previous session a classmate had introduced the notion of 'the right stuff' to describe the various elements that contributed to a leader's success. This seemed to strike a chord with the Professor for he had used that concept as the basis for a new project, with individuals being allocated different aspects of the right stuff to further research and explore.

Karl got mindset. Or more precisely, he had been asked to be prepared at the next session to describe the mindset of an effective leader.

At first he had scoffed at what seemed to be such a simple task but, as he delved more deeply into it, he realized that it was far from easy to describe how the best leaders think; or at least to communicate it in such a way as would make sense to his classmates. He knew that no two leaders would, or indeed should, think exactly alike but he wanted to capture the common elements found in the mindset of all effective managers.

Doing that, he felt, required him to consider three related aspects: how leaders think about life in general, the scale of their ambitions and how they specifically view the leadership role.

When it came to general outlook Karl always had been a great believer in the power of positive thinking and recent years had only strengthened that belief. He was a natural optimist who recognized that, if he allowed himself to become consumed by negativity, the likelihood of bad things happening increased dramatically. That is not to say he was blinkered to reality but he understood that if he lost hope, then he was finished; he didn't need to read *The Secret* or watch Dr Phil in order to understand the laws of attraction. Staying upbeat had always been his way and touched everything he did.

Having a positive outlook, he firmly believed, also was crucial to success as a manager. He didn't mean the kind of nonsense you see in some companies where the leader spends half the time running about waving his arms in the air chanting some uplifting mantra. Nor was he talking about the sort of blind optimism or self-delusional approach promoted by some, whereby positive thinking for managers is seen as a panacea for all ills. No, that philosophy he believed, to use a football analogy, was the equivalent of the 'Hail-Mary pass' mentality – whereby leaders lived on false hope alone.

That was a recipe for disaster, not success.

Instead he felt that all managers had to be realists too by anticipating, and indeed preparing for, worst-case scenarios. They could not live in Cloud Cuckoo Land. That said, it was a leader's overall mindset that mattered most and the more positive the outlook they held, the greater the likelihood of success. This was not because he imagined for one minute that a manager got what she wanted simply because she wished it so, or that, as some of the self-help gurus alleged, one could magically achieve great things just by visualizing the desired outcome. That was a sham. Instead, he believed in the power of positive thinking for two reasons.

First with an upbeat mindset, leaders are better equipped mentally to face down the challenges they encounter so that means they are less likely to throw in the towel, which of itself helps them to achieve more. Second employees feed off the positive vibes and this helps to bring out the best in them as well, with the result that they too push harder for better results. It was this collective effort, he believed, that delivered the success, not some form of mental hocus-pocus.

He therefore knew that having an overall positive attitude was the first critical component of the leader's mindset that he needed to describe during his talk later that evening. That box was ticked.

As he watched the children chasing each other around the playground he noticed how one over-protective mother seemed to really smother her little boy. He wondered how that might play out over a lifetime. It also reminded him of how he had been greatly influenced, as everyone surely is, by his parents and although they had served as role models for him in very many respects, in some ways they had unwittingly highlighted pitfalls to avoid.

His father, for instance, had been a man who had lived for his family and he had many great traits that Karl admired. All the same, he had one failing, if that's the word – not unusual in that generation – because he placed strong limitations on what he felt he could achieve in life. His father was risk-averse, believing that someone was born with a certain set of skills and competencies and they either had a talent for something or they didn't. There was little point, in his dad's mind at least, in seeking to develop skills that you could never really master; the potential for failure was too high. This influenced how he viewed life in general and was captured nicely in his oft-repeated phrase, "stick to the knitting, son."

Karl, on the other hand, didn't see the same ceiling in terms of his potential, nor did he fear the unknown – he would never have started his own business had he done so. Sure, he didn't delude himself that he could become an Olympic medalist just because he set that goal, but he did feel that he could get better at things, at least to the extent where he was in a position to compete effectively and that was what mattered. Challenging himself or taking a calculated risk took guts but led to greater rewards in the end.

This was, he believed, a second important feature of the leader's mindset that he needed to convey later that evening. In his view, the best leaders weren't afraid to reach for the stars, even if they understood the need to stay within our own galaxy.

The third aspect of the leader's mindset that he felt it was important to communicate was how the best managers he had met viewed the leadership role itself. He felt very strongly about the importance of the link between how a leader thinks and what they actually do, so he was keen to describe that feature in meaningful terms to his classmates.

First off, successful leaders, it seemed to him, recognize that attitudes to work today are radically different, so they make a big effort to apply innovative approaches in order to bring the best out of people. They really seem to get the point that whereas just telling employees what to do might be easier, it doesn't get the best results over the long term.

In particular as he reflected on the one or two great managers he had worked for, he remembered how passionate they had been about engaging their employees, really involving them in meaningful decision-making and using two-way communication channels to create an open and trusting environment. He would sum up this third feature of the leader's mindset in words he had recently read from Ken Blanchard, that respected leadership expert and author, when he said:

In the past, a leader was a boss. Today's leaders must be partners with their people; they can no longer lead solely based on positional power.

As Karl watched the apprehensive mother shadowing her little boy whilst he climbed the steps to the slide – hands at the ready to form a makeshift maternal safety net – it was these snippets of his own mindset, and that of other leaders he admired, that he was trying to structure into a coherent manner for his talk in a few hours. But how to bring it all together, that was the challenge?

He saw the child run from the bottom of the slide to the brightly painted little wooden boat in the activity area and, like a bolt out of the blue, an idea came to him.

He reached for his Blackberry and did some searching online until he found what he was looking for. Then, he prepared an email merge to all his classmates under the subject line, 'Would you reply to the following job advert?' In the body of the email, he placed the following text, nothing more:

Men wanted for hazardous journey, small wages, bitter cold, long months of complete darkness, constant danger, safe return doubtful, honor and recognition in case of success.

He ended the message with the words 'answers required tonight in class,' and he chuckled to himself as he pressed send. No doubt, there would be some scratching of heads when they got this.

Later that evening, as he stood in front of his classmates, he asked how many of them would apply based on the advert.

A few jokingly enquired what the pay would be, and one of the girls took slight umbrage as to why only men were invited to apply – the smile on her face letting everyone know she was not, in truth, that uptight. One member of the group did say that he would love to go for it, except it sounded too much like the crappy career he already had, but the glare from the Professor had let that particular individual know that his repeated attempts at humor were gaining little traction.

In the end none of his classmates seemed overly keen given the description of what was on offer.

Karl explained that his email had referred to an advertisement placed in British newspapers by Sir Ernest Shackleton prior to his expedition to the South Pole in 1914. "Over 5,000 men actually replied to that ad," he continued, "and 27 of them were selected. In August that year, they set off from England under Shackleton's command on an Antarctic expedition with the intention of being the first to complete a transcontinental crossing.

"From the moment their ship *Endurance* entered the Wedell Sea off the Antarctic Peninsula in early 1915," he continued, "anything that could have possibly gone wrong with the mission did so. *Endurance* became trapped in ice and was later crushed by its force and the group remained stranded for months on ice floes suffering one unimaginable challenge after the other, including having to shoot and then eat the sled dogs they had all grown so fond of, as well as undertaking a seven-day sea voyage in flimsy lifeboats to reach the uninhabited Elephant Island, which still lay beyond the possibility of rescue."

Karl explained how, despite the hopelessness of their position, Shackleton's optimism never waned during the endless months of uncertainty. Staring death in the face, he still did not quit.

"As a last throw of the dice," he added, "Shackleton and several crew members left the main group and undertook a treacherous voyage in a small boat, crossing 800 miles of the roughest seas on earth in order to reach the nearest inhabited island, South Georgia: a feat later described, without exaggeration, as the equivalent of finding a needle in a haystack. Then having landed on the wrong side of that island, he and his small crew had to cross over the uncharted and dangerous mountainous interior to reach the whaling station, from where rescue for his remaining men would later be launched. He had promised them he would return and return he did on August 30, 1916. Not one member of the party was lost.

"Shackleton undoubtedly had many great qualities as a leader," said Karl, "but he himself placed optimism at the top of the list of attributes that saw him through the ordeal, followed by patience, and imagination. Without his never-say-die mindset it is probable that he and all his men would have met a cold and painful death. When asked later how he had coped with such unrelenting challenges, Shackleton simply replied, 'Difficulties are just things to overcome, after all.'

"Thankfully," added Karl, "none of us have to face such a series of seemingly insurmountable challenges every day, but mindset still matters for all of us and particularly so during challenging economic times such as these. The best leaders always have an upbeat and determined outlook, which contributes to their ability to effectively lead others.

"No, they don't come running across the car park every morning waving their arms in the air chanting some uplifting mantra, nor do they wear tee-shirts with *Carpe Diem* written on it. But, by nature, they are optimists who recognize that, if they allow themselves to become consumed by negativity, what chance is there for everyone else around them? That is not to say they are blinkered to reality, but they understand that if they lose hope, so too will their people.

"Tonight I would like to describe for you what I truly believe are the three essential components of the leader's mindset ..."

First, have a definite, clear practical ideal; a goal, an objective. Second, have the necessary means to achieve your ends: wisdom, money, materials, and methods. Third, adjust all your means to that end.

Aristotle

MOON TALKING

"No way in hell, buddy, no way in hell. We never went to the freakin' moon. Simply never happened, my friend. The whole thing was rigged. Can't you remember? We were being owned by the Russians in the Space Race at the time and NASA had to do something mega to put it up to the Reds. So, they made it all up. It was faked. Yup, just like the government always does, they played us like dumb-ass fools."

This guy is a total quack, how on earth did we end up talking to him?

Inner Voice is right. How did I end up stuck in this bizarre conversation? Well, maybe, if I am honest, it isn't all that hard to figure out how this has happened. Throwing back those eight beers might have had something to do with the fact that I am now sitting next to a guy who is practically foaming at the mouth.

And he is not alone either by the sound of things.

"You're damn right, man," shouts another guy at the far side of the bar, who obviously has good hearing functionality but seemingly little else going on inside his head. "If we had actually been to the moon, then why is it going to take us at least until 2020 to go back? I read somewhere that NASA said they had forgotten how to get there. Forgotten? Hah, that's a bit rich seeing as we were never actually up there in the first place."

There is no point in even asking him where he heard that. No doubt, it is likely to have come from such a reliable source as the *National Enquirer*.

"Have you ever heard of the Van Halen radiation belt?" says the first lunar expert, spraying half his mouthful of beer on me as he does so.

The lunacy around me is really starting to spread now.

"You mean, the 'Van Allen' radiation belt, is it?" I reply.

"Yup, that's what I said."

"Actually, you ..." Oh, what would be the point in finishing that sentence? I think it is probably best just to let him spew some more nonsense; although I am pretty sure that what he is about to say will come from way out there in left field.

"To get to the moon, I heard that those guys would have had to pass through that Van Halen belt thingy. Only one slight problem though, bud, if astronauts had actually travelled through it, they would have been fried – like pieces of KFC – so there's no way in hell we could have sent them through it twice in a tin can and got them back home safely. It was all a massive hoax.

"Where have you been for the past couple of decades? Sure, Kissinger even admitted that the whole thing was faked: he said that Stanley Kubrick filmed the 'moon landings' in a specially designed studio. You can find out all about it on the web, if you don't believe me."

He didn't disappoint, did he? Never mind left field, that came from a different ball park entirely. If he wasn't so scary, he might actually be funny.

"Yea," says yet another guy joining in as the madness continues to seep around the bar, "you can tell the Apollo landings were phony just by looking at the photographs or the video. Kubrick did a lousy job, got the lighting angles all wrong. Look, in one shot, you can actually see the American flag flapping away in the breeze, as if there was any wind on the moon. Some idiot must have left a door open in the studio or something. Plus, didn't you hear that people watching it 'live' in Australia said they saw one of the astronauts kick a Coke bottle when he walked across the moon?

"What's more, have you seen the press conference with the crew when they 'returned?' They didn't look too happy I can tell you, not like you should be if you HAD just travelled to the moon and back. Do you get what I'm saying? And, hey, they couldn't even answer whether they saw any stars or not when they were down on the surface. Gimme a break, how can anyone believe it actually happened for real?"

They are really starting to come out of the woodwork now. It won't be long before these three loons actually start barking at the moon, I fear. Time for me to go.

And fast.

I only came into Molly's tonight to have a chat with my new friend Bob, to run a couple of ideas by him for an article I am writing, but he doesn't work weekends apparently. Now I know why. They must open the doors to the local nuthouse on a Saturday night or something. I made the mistake of staying around for a few drinks and look what I have gotten myself into.

As I finish my beer quickly I am still trying to figure out how the heck we got onto all this moon gibberish anyway ... oh, I remember now. It's all coming back to me.

A few minutes ago we were actually talking about something reasonably sensible, about how people should set goals to help them achieve great things. I made what has clearly turned out to be the major mistake of saying that, when President Kennedy said, "I believe that this nation should commit itself to achieving the goal, before this decade is out, of landing a man on the Moon and returning him safely to the Earth ...", he is rightly credited with having set a target that lifted the aspirations of a generation and energized a nation.

I had only used that particular example because I was trying to make the point that the 'right' goals could really lift people, could get everyone excited and working in the same direction. I was simply trying to explain that, to this day, the concept of proactive goal-setting is seen as an important element in personal and business success.

But I hadn't allowed for the fact that I must have been transported onto the set of *One Flew Over the Cuckoo's Nest* or something. These psychos around me somehow must have only heard my reference to the moon. Then they were off.

Downing the last of my beer, I know I need to leave pronto before we move on to any more conspiracy theories. Come to think of it, it is likely to only be a matter of time before one of them remembers that I also mentioned JFK a while back and that will definitely kick off some more insanity. I am out of here.

I start to walk the few blocks towards my apartment.

Actually, change of plan.

I think I will hit my own local for a good steak and a glass of vino. I realize that the advisable thing would probably be to go straight home immediately, but sensible and Saturday night never sat well together with me. Anyway, I'm hungry. At least I know that I can dine in peace in Dylan's and watch the TV without any fear of catching the psychosis bug.

Sitting here at the bar watching the sports news I am listening to some Head Coach talk about his views on the season ahead, the targets he has set with the team and the various milestones along the way. He gets the hamster going in my head again and I think back to the earlier conversation in Molly's.

No, not the nonsensical part, but the bit where I was talking about the importance of goals. The point I had wanted to make, before we drifted into the twilight zone, was how I believe that the setting of goals is important, in life and in work, because it begins to translate vague hopes into concrete results against which actions can then be directed.

I start making some notes on the napkin because, despite my brain being well and truly doused in alcohol, there are some good ideas floating around up there tonight; nothing worse than having great revelations that I can't remember tomorrow.

Listening to Coach in the background, unfortunately – now that I have figured out which team he's from and how they have underperformed over the last few years – I think what he has come up with are, in truth, more wishes than goals. This reminds me that I have some reservations attached to the whole goal-setting thing.

Now, don't get me wrong, goals are good, for sure, if and when the goals are good. What I mean by that is that setting unrealistic goals can do more harm than good. Too many people today, driven by a lot of self-help claptrap, set improbable goals for themselves, given their talents and the level of effort they are prepared to put into realizing them. *I want to be famous and the like.* When those goals are not achieved it can have a negative rather than a positive impact.

I think this principle applies in a work context too. Managers also must be careful when setting business goals – if they want to be effective, that is – in terms of how they are devised and structured, because badly-designed goals can be worse than having no goals at all; they can lead everyone in a direction that is counterproductive. I have seen many companies establish goals – for example, in terms of revenue – which although achieved were not of real value because the costs generated in hitting those targets meant that the increased revenue did not translate proportionally to the bottom line.

Tucking into my steak, my mind wanders for a bit.

I think again of the big point I would have made back there in Molly's, which was that goal orientation and effective management, for me, undoubtedly go hand in hand, but with the 'good goal' provisions in mind. I really do believe that goals are critical for leaders in all aspects of their lives.

First and foremost they need to set realistic personal goals, which stretch them for sure, but are also within their capability to realize because they can't just rely on positive thinking alone to get them where they want to go.

With regard to work, successful leaders also need a clear view of what they are trying to achieve, but they must make sure that these goals have the effect of adding real value to the business.

I tune back into Coach, and to be fair, even though I think he is a tad optimistic with regard to his team's goals, he is still making some valid points about the goal-setting process he adopts. What he is saying about how he goes about creating goals is interesting because I think it has applications too in a work context.

A few boisterous late-night drinkers arrive in and it's a bit hard to make out what he is saying. I ask Ron to turn up the sound so I can hear Coach:

I always try to include my players in defining the targets in the first place because after all, they are the ones who have to put in the hard yards out there on the field to achieve them. The more involved they are in agreeing our aims, the more likely they will put that extra effort in. I also try to break the season's goals down into shorter focused sub-goals; this helps us identify 'little wins' that encourage further effort. Another important step I take is to get everyone to publicly commit to attaining the goals because breaking promises to their team mates is not something most people like to do.

These are certainly relevant points he is making and funnily enough I think they apply just as well for a leader when setting goals for a team in the workplace. Coach continues:

To sustain momentum one of my tasks is to offer continuous encouragement and motivation for the guys, even more so when we suffer a defeat or have a lousy stint at the office. But it's not really about me holding their hands at the end of the day. I am a big believer in letting them monitor and evaluate their own progress; they know what they did well, where things went wrong, who was to blame and so on and they can work out how to fix the things that need fixing. It's very much a two-way process and not just about me telling them what's wrong and how to put things right.

Sure we fight about problems and solutions but that's a good thing. At least it tells me that they are committed to what we are trying to do as a team. It says they care enough to argue.

Once we have a game plan in place, in many ways, my job is to get the hell out of the way and let them put it into action. I support and guide from the sidelines.

Coach is making a lot of sense, but I think there is one limitation to what he is saying if those principles were to be applied in organizations. For the inclusive approach to goal-setting and achievement to work, the right team needs to be in place: right in the sense of attitude, but also with regard to individual and collective skills. No point in trying to set goals with employees who lack commitment to the cause, or in allowing individuals who don't have the necessary talents to self-assess their own performance.

When the team isn't in the zone, the leader has to carry more of the load in terms of both setting, and then in monitoring, progress towards the goals. Still, the collective route is a good one when the team can step up to the mark.

As I enjoy the last of my wine it never ceases to amaze me that there are lessons to be learned in the strangest of places. Maybe for my next book on leadership I can use some of what Coach has said in terms of goal-setting. I spend a couple of minutes checking my notes on the napkin; at least they are fairly legible, a major achievement given the not too healthy state I am in.

That done, I think it's probably a good time to head for the hills, because experience tells me that if I have another drink things will likely start to get messy.

Turning the key in my apartment door I have a final thought on the goal issue. Once business goals are set, I believe, effective managers excel at sustaining buy-in for them, so much so that I have often been quite surprised at just how much employees come to see the goals as being their own. The result is that those who work for good managers tend to feel part of something bigger than themselves and view the achievement of organizational goals and satisfying their own needs and aspirations as being compatible, not contradictory.

I add those points to my now pretty full napkin.

And as my head hits the pillow I just know it is going to be sore tomorrow.

*The single biggest problem in communication
is the illusion that it has taken place.*

George Bernard Shaw

EMPTY WORDS

"As you know, we are facing into a mega-busy time with this important product launch coming up at the end of the month, so I would urge that it be all hands on deck for the next few weeks before we go live ... there is a lot of prep-work to be done, across all divisions not just my own, and I am not sure whether we have the bandwidth to cope with it, unless we all pull together ... so I called this meeting today to see what you guys can bring to the table to help operationalize this one ..."

Mike cringed as he heard the words. And he wasn't alone either.

There was a real sense of discomfort in the conference room as the jargon rolled from Milli's tongue in glorious monotone. A weird sensation took hold too, as if the heat had been turned up, with everyone feeling slightly warmer due to their collective embarrassment. How could anyone, Mike thought, be so limited in their ability to communicate as to stand up in front of a group of executives – his colleagues – and mouth that sort of nonsense?

'Bandwidth,' what the heck did that actually mean anyway?

'Bring to the table,' who uses stuff like that these days?

'Operationalize,' is he for real?

Was this a scene from *The Office*, or something, Mike wondered?

It wasn't unfortunately. This was really happening.

Yet for all the trauma of having to sit through another of Milli's lame-ass 'meetings,' which in reality were just opportunities for him to talk at people, Mike still found it somewhat interesting to watch the faces of those in attendance as they threw despairing glances at one another, only barely concealing their annoyance. If the CEO hadn't been there Milli undoubtedly would have been given a fairly rough ride. His subordinates might not be in a position to tell him what they thought, but given half a chance, some of this senior group would have had no such qualms.

It was an open secret that most people around that table struggled to understand how Milli held down such a senior position in the business, given his poor communication skills and penchant for waffle; although, to be fair, he always looked the part and was very talented in other ways, which obviously had compensated. But he could probably have achieved so much more had he just worked on improving his ability to communicate. Unfortunately he didn't seem interested in making that effort.

In the early days when Milli first joined the company, Mike had genuinely made an effort to build bridges with him, as he did when any new associate started. But he never seemed to get anywhere with Milli. It was like coming up against a brick wall.

On one occasion over a beer he had even tried to subtly highlight the communication issues – in a constructive manner, peer to peer – but his genuine attempt to offer support had been slapped down, with Milli countering that it was Mike's fear of being overshadowed that was driving his 'so-called' concern. Milli was not, Mike had quickly learned, the most collaborative individual on the planet and everything seemed to be about one-upmanship where he was concerned.

So in the end, out of frustration as much as anything else, Mike had come up with the nickname 'Milli' for him. Yes, he knew it was a very schoolyardish thing to do, but he really couldn't help himself. The guy just drove him around the twist. At first not everyone on the senior team got the reference but that all changed once Mike gave them the background.

You see, Milli Vanilli had been on their way to becoming musical icons. Well, for a fleeting moment, they had been, at least. Having burst onto the pop scene in the late 1980s the duo with the funny hairstyles celebrated a few chart-topping hits and won a couple of Grammy awards. They were going places, or so it seemed. Only one slight problem, though: they couldn't actually sing, at least not very well, nor indeed could they play any instruments to the standard required.

Then during one 'live' performance, a jammed tape machine at the back of the stage revealed them to be miming, which led to a major backlash from both media and fans alike, after which they quickly faded into oblivion. They had been exposed as fakes.

And ever since the christening all agreed that Milli was a perfect choice of nickname for their colleague because, in a sense, he too was only miming when it came to communication.

N ow Mike didn't think of himself as being without fault – far from it – nor did he pretend to be some sort of master communicator but he did know that he was streets ahead of Milli when it came to interacting with others. Whilst Mike recognized that effective communication lay at the heart of any positive relationship, Milli seemed not to grasp this fundamental concept, or if he did, he had a strange view as to what good communication actually entailed.

Yes, Milli was often the first to pay lip service to its importance, particularly around the boss, but in practice he seemed for someone at his level to be lousy at it and worse still, completely oblivious as to his own shortcomings. Instead of mastering the art of communication he was prone to mutilating it, as again on this occasion. His failings as a communicator were many and varied for sure, but Mike believed they were caused in large part by Milli's lack of the right stuff, especially self-awareness.

When it came to interacting with others Mike was guided by what his dad – someone who was a master communicator, at least in a work setting – had told him many times: namely that regular and structured communication with employees, individually and collectively, was the oil that kept the engine running smoothly. Without it, things tended to seize up in some shape or form.

Still his father had always qualified that particular nugget by emphasizing how important it was not to focus solely on the quantity of communication, but to be equally concerned with its quality too.

Over recent years Mike had noticed how Milli really struggled with both aspects at times. Frequently he failed to communicate enough, so he fell down on the quantity side, but even if he did get the amount of communication right, its quality often was poor for a number of reasons.

First off, Milli had a tendency to over-rely on written communications with the goal seemingly being more to cover his own ass than anything else. Mike received so many emails from him in the course of a day that he no longer paid attention to many of them and he left it to his assistant to spot the relevant ones and ignore the rest. Not ideal, clearly, but unavoidable when he already had hundreds of emails from various sources coming through every week.

Of course Mike understood very well that written forms of communication had their place, but for him, there was no substitute for meaningful personal interaction.

Even when Milli did give 'face-time' – another of his silly labels – to people, he had substantial problems and seemed not to fully register that the manner in which he transmitted a message was just as important as the message itself. He didn't really seem to get the need to balance content (*words)* and context (*tone and body language),* or at least not to the extent that someone in his position should have done. As a result he frequently mismatched what he said with how he said it and his style of communication often served to decrease the attention span of his listeners and reduce the impact of what he was trying to say.

Mike, on the other hand, had learned some basic but vital lessons very early in his working life about the importance of getting the content-context mix right. As a teenager, he had held down a summer job in a local pizza restaurant on Cape Cod, and even at that young age, he could see that certain people just didn't know how to communicate.

In particular the owner, a real shouter, was always having a crisis about something or other; and when he did, his face began to turn purple and a little vein on his forehead started throbbing. This was quite a source of amusement generally for the employees, with some calling their boss the 'Purple People-eater' when he got like that; others said he looked like Barney's psycho brother, a reference to the popular children's cartoon character that had just come on the scene at that time.

And when the owner had a go at Mike back then – sometimes with good reason, for he was a bit of a slacker in his teenage years – he just could not seem to take his eyes off that vein. The context – lots of screaming, shouting and facial contortions – would cause him to miss half of what his boss was saying. All he could think of was what would happen if the vein actually burst. Although he didn't realize it at the time it was an early lesson in how not to communicate: don't ever let context overshadow content.

In terms of the content side of things, Milli was prone to taking too long to get to the point and was a real windbag on occasion, smattering his sentences with badly chosen words, meaningless metaphors and cringe worthy jargon that pushed the patience of his audience to the limit.

His difficulties with content were made worse by what he repeatedly did with context; he cocked-up in this area because he missed the point about the emotional impact of tone and body language which led to a multitude of sins, like his monotone voice or wooden body posture. He did try to use positive hand gestures and movements but it always seemed a bit robotic somehow.

To add to his problems he tended to be a bad listener too. So not only was he a poor sender of messages but he wasn't the best at receiving them either.

The combined effect of Milli's repetitive, negative behaviors meant that he did not reach others at anything other than a superficial level and in reality, he encouraged the listener to tune out not in, losing some or all of the impact of his message in the process. In truth, Mike felt a bit sorry for him because it was not a case that he never had valid things to say – he was a bright guy – but time and time again, he had seen how the manner in which Milli said things weakened, or even killed, the power of the points he wanted to make.

But what could be done if the guy was totally up his own rear-end and unwilling to take advice? Ultimately you can't save people from themselves.

"... I really want to make sure that all our people are singing from the same hymnsheet about this new product coming on stream

... at the moment, I feel there's a bit of cat-herding going on ... making a mess of this launch isn't going to happen on my watch ..."

As Mike sat there in the meeting room with the droning continuing in the background, it just seemed impossible that someone as senior as Milli could understand so little about the sender-receiver loop when it came to face-to-face communications.

Being a big movie buff Mike's wandering mind thought again of a great line from the classic film *Cool Hand Luke*. In one powerful scene, the evil warden, the Captain, beats Luke, played by Paul Newman, and knocks him to the ground. Then standing menacingly over Luke, the Captain utters the memorable words, "What we have here is ... failure to communicate."

Milli, a.k.a. Steve Howley, constantly failed to communicate.

Nothing is softer or more flexible than water,
yet nothing can resist it.

Lao Tzu

STYLE AND SUBSTANCE

Richard Douglas loved life in the Marines.

Well it would probably be more accurate to say that he had both loved and hated the experience. At the time he had been very proud to serve his country alongside men he trusted and admired, some of whom were later to become lifelong friends. That was certainly the high point of his time in the Forces.

He had hated it simply because it was Hell.

That's what Vietnam was like. No other way to describe it. No rose-tinted descriptions colored by the passage of time. It was one enduring nightmare.

When he had volunteered to serve in '67 he assumed he knew what he was letting himself in for but as it turned out, he had absolutely no idea of what lay ahead. It was beyond the capacity of words to describe what he had endured physically and mentally out there. Yet he had served with distinction, rising to the rank of Captain until he was wounded in action in '69, for which he later received the Purple Heart.

His time in 'Nam, though, had taught him many valuable lessons about life, the most important being that it was precious and fleeting. Frequently, when under attack, or out on night patrol, where a silent hidden enemy could emerge from the shadows at any time without warning, he had vowed that if he made it through the war alive, he would live every day of the rest of his life to the full. Not a minute would he waste.

As he now sat in The Madison reminiscing with the old friend seated opposite, that promise, he hoped, had been kept.

He also had learned what he thought at the time were critical lessons about leading others. For the most part, he had witnessed one style of leadership in action from the superiors under whom he served: often a brutal, aggressive form of leadership, designed to keep the men in line and to push them to do what they would normally never have done. It worked, simply because soldiers believed that the tougher the leader, the more likely he would get them through to the other side unscathed.

For Richard leadership and toughness, therefore, were two peas in a pod.

After he was discharged and when his leg wound had fully healed – or at least had mended to the extent where he was left with a life-long limp and constant stiffness – he took a job as a lowly pen-pusher in the claims section of a growing insurance company. Not much reward for having placed his neck on the line he remembered thinking that first day he entered the building and took his seat at one of the neatly aligned rows of desks. But he had ambitions.

He may not have had any qualifications, other than his high school diploma, but he did have an unrelenting drive and a phenomenal work ethic, putting himself through night school to achieve first a Business degree, and then later a Master's. Slowly but steadily he climbed the ranks, initially in the Personal Markets Division, then shifting to the Commercial side, with stints in all key functional areas until after 20 years, he became the top man in the company, one of the leading nationwide insurers.

His first taste of leadership in the firm, however, had been far from auspicious and it certainly didn't serve as a pointer to the bright future that lay ahead of him. After about two years he was appointed head of a small team of claims adjusters; the previous leader had been around for a long time – was almost part of the furniture – but he had suddenly jumped ship to join a rival firm.

Mostly the team was performing well and Richard was promoted largely because he was the longest serving member at that point, and so next in line, rather than for any spark of leadership he might or might not have shown. It was a bit like the Marines in that sense he joked at the time: when one dropped, another fool put himself in harm's way.

On taking over Richard came out with all guns blazing, way too hard and far too enthusiastically, as it turned out. He had been eager to establish himself quickly, to prove to the team, and others, that he could be just as good, if not better, than his predecessor. So he decided to shake things up a bit, to let them all know that there was a new Sergeant in the platoon, so to speak.

One of the areas he targeted for change was how the workload was organized and distributed between the team members. He believed that the adjusters had far too much freedom over how they planned their week. The old system might have worked well under the previous leader but he felt that more structure would be good for everyone; there was untapped productivity in the team and he knew how to release it. And doing so would get him noticed.

His first action therefore was to introduce a new reporting system, whereby each adjuster had to provide a work plan to him at the beginning of every week. It didn't sit well at all with the team, but despite their protests, Richard held firm. He was not for turning, he assured them, so they had better get used to it. In any case he believed that they would come to appreciate the benefits of the system over time. They didn't.

He had hoped the change would raise productivity and increase the general quality of the work but a month or so after the introduction of the new regime, there had been problems with missed deadlines, which had rarely happened before. Richard felt this was happening because a couple of the guys were intentionally dragging their feet with the altered system, deliberately slowing down the pace of work just to stymie his changes. They were fronting up to him.

He fought back and challenged them head-on, which led to a number of heated arguments developing. Every day became a struggle. One thing for sure, he felt at the time, there was no damn way that he was going to allow himself to be beaten by what he saw as outright insubordination. He continued to lay down the law, which of course only served to make things worse.

Naturally the then Head of the Department soon became aware of the problems – if nothing else, he could hear the raised voices on occasion – and eventually he sat Richard down to discuss the situation with him. Had that little *tête-à-tête* taken another track, or had his boss been a less understanding individual, Richard's career might have taken a very different trajectory; a fact he was never to forget in his future dealings with employees in the years ahead.

His manager started a process that day that was to see him become a life-long mentor and friend to Richard. He also provided him with his first major leadership lesson in the world of work, one which, as he now sat in the restaurant looking back on those days, Richard knew had set him up for success.

His boss had opened that conversation with a simple statement.

Management, he had explained, or the style of management to be adopted in any given situation, was about avoiding the extremes. On the one hand, he said, in order to lead others effectively, Richard couldn't be passive because any leadership role required tough decisions and actions, the severity and importance of which increased with progression up the ladder. So there was no place for shrinking violets in the world of management.

Yet shifting to the other extreme entirely by adopting an aggressive, my-way-or-the-highway approach was equally ineffective. Richard might be able to win these immediate battles, his boss had conceded, but ultimately people did not perform to their best when coerced into doing something, so he would lose the war in the long run.

Finding a middle way therefore was what effective leaders did. They negotiated a path between being too soft or too hard and they had the ability to adopt flexible leadership styles within that middle ground. That was the key to lasting success in management, he advised.

It was a message with which, at first, Richard felt strongly inclined to disagree. He countered with many examples from his military experience where tough-guy approaches had worked to good effect. In response, his boss, also a former Marine – albeit from an earlier time – and clearly someone with lots of patience, made another simple statement that Richard remembered for many years. Leadership, he had emphasized, was all about context, so it was important to compare like with like.

War was ultimately about life and death and styles of leadership needed to reflect that, plus the accepted culture within the army was one of a top-down approach. Men would shut up and follow the leader whom they felt would most likely keep them alive, regardless of how aggressive or dictatorial that leader's style might be.

But work was not about such stark realities, his boss had pointed out, and because of that, a more sophisticated approach was required to get the best from people. Managers therefore needed to adjust their style to fit the circumstances faced and had to find a way to exercise their legitimate power without having to resort to aggression or intimidation. At the same time, he assured Richard, being more subtle did not mean being weak.

It did, however, mean being smart.

Some time passed before Richard fully recognized the importance of that lesson but with experience, he began to understand how the best leaders had the capacity to deftly adjust their approach in response to different people or events and how they could manage diverse situations without losing their cool. It was a form of juggling act whereby they needed to decide how much *direction* to give people and how much *control* to exercise over their actions, as opposed to how much to *involve* people in the decision-making process and how much *autonomy* to give them in the completion of their duties.

Certain leaders, he noticed over time, applied too much direction and control, whereas others gave too much freedom and autonomy. Some were too passive at times, whilst others were overly aggressive. It was always about finding that elusive middle ground and he spent a lot of time in those early days trying to learn how to get the balance right.

He began to see too that there were a number of factors that influenced the approach he needed to adopt. One was the nature of the employees he was dealing with. If the team was highly motivated and engaged, then naturally he needed to lead them with a different style than he would have done with a less engaged unit. Various individuals within the team also needed flexible approaches and the ability and/or willingness of an employee to deliver what was expected of them always would determine how he needed to respond as a manager. Then he saw that different situations, events and problems required varied responses.

These all seemed like elementary lessons as he now looked back on them but at the time, having only ever experienced one style of leadership, the subtlety required to lead effectively in the business world was a revelation.

With time he started to understand that flexibility was the key, but he also recognized how this was easier said than done; the ability to be flexible required him to have the right personal attributes and skills so that he could first identify, and then apply, the best style. Richard saw that he needed to sort out his failings, such as his extremely short fuse, if he was to make it as an outstanding leader, so he spent a lot of time in those early years working on those personal characteristics that he felt might be holding him back.

During his night classes he also developed a better understanding of leadership in theory but such was his love of simplicity, he felt it was all over-complicated; too many models or approaches, all essentially saying the same thing was how he saw it. So he developed his own basic framework of leadership styles, based on the *direction-control* and *involvement-autonomy* dynamic, one which was to serve him well for the rest of his career.

He understood that the more *direction* and *control* he exercised, the less *involvement* and *autonomy* his employees would have, so in effect they were polar opposites and if he was high on one, he naturally would be low on the other. The different styles of leadership he defined therefore were determined by where he placed the emphasis; and that could be influenced by the levels of mutual trust and respect between him and his team – the higher these were, the more likely he was to involve his people in decision-making or to allow them greater autonomy.

He captured all this into three distinct styles of leadership that he could adopt for any given situation. He saw them almost as a sliding scale that he needed to cleverly move back and forth upon, depending on what the situation or individual called for.

The first style he described as *Steering*. Sometimes, it was clear that he had to exercise high direction and control over his team as a whole, or on individuals within it. He needed to 'steer' them in the direction he wanted them to go. It was an essential style, he believed, when faced with individual or collective under-performance, when quick decisions or prompt action was required or indeed when plans had to be implemented that were not open to debate.

Although it required him to be firm and even direct with people at times, he had learned that it did not mean being aggressive because that type of approach was always counterproductive. Acting like an asshole was not part of any style of leadership, or at least not one that delivered the best results.

The second style he called *Engaging*. He recognized that his goal with any team had to be to work hard to reduce direction and control and to increase involvement and autonomy because if he didn't do so, in effect he was creating employees who acted like robots – they would not use their own initiative. He realized that this style could be applied in simple ways by including people in decision-making or in allowing them to propose solutions to given problems.

For most of the time, he made an effort to try to adopt the engaging style because he knew that, by its very nature, it helped to build the engagement levels of his employees.

The third style he described as *Facilitating*. On some occasions, particularly with top-performing teams or individuals, he saw that he had to be willing to give them high levels of involvement and autonomy. As a leader there were times when he needed to take a step backwards and to trust his people to make the right moves. He always remained in charge, of course, but he had to notice and then respond to those occasions when his people were ready to be essentially self-managing.

Richard believed that these three styles and the ability to move seamlessly back and forth between them provided him with the flexibility necessary to cope with the nuances of work life. The fact that he also devoted a lot of time to developing his personal attributes, such as his level of self-control, and to enhancing his skills, like his ability to communicate, meant that, over time, his capacity as a manager grew and this in turn helped him deliver outstanding results.

Of course he was far from perfect but most of the time, he got it right and this helped him rise quickly through the ranks.

A s I used to tell people," Richard said to the elderly man seated opposite him in the restaurant, "I am a bit like a chameleon. I try to adapt my style to fit whatever situation or person I am faced with. I make a conscious – and that word is very important – decision as to what leadership style is going to work best based on the scenario facing me. And it is thanks to you that I ended up thinking like that ..."

Whilst he was sitting in The Madison waiting for his son Mike to arrive for lunch, it had been a gentle tap on the shoulder that had sent Richard on this trip down memory lane.

He had turned to see his old friend and mentor – now well into his 90s – standing at his side. Then as they sat together and thought again of distant days, Richard had recalled his first steps into management, the struggle to find his feet in the role and how he had gradually developed his own approach. He was still grateful for that early leadership lesson from the old Marine seated across the table and indeed for his ongoing support over many years.

In response the elderly man reminded him of the Marine Corps motto: *Semper Fidelis*, 'always faithful'. "Theirs was," he said, "a brotherhood that lasted for life. There was no such thing as an ex-Marine."

Richard smiled at this, and as he looked into those still bright eyes, he was thankful that, way back in those early days, he had the sense to listen to someone who knew infinitely more about management than he did. And he was proud too that he had developed his own capabilities as a leader to a level where, even though he was now retired, he still was known affectionately as 'Boss.'

The most intense conflicts, if overcome, leave behind a sense of security and calm that is not easily disturbed. It is just these intense conflicts and their conflagration which are needed to produce valuable and lasting results.

Carl Gustav Jung

FIGHTS AND FLIGHTS

I don't get paid from the neck up.

"I don't get paid from the neck up." Heather Gardner repeated the sentence quietly to herself, shaking her head in disbelief. And as she watched the raindrops slide in odd formations down the greasy window, she knew that those words captured everything. That one response perfectly summed up the mess her company was in. A strong sense of despondency hit her as the car swung in under the portico.

"Ms. Gardner, Ms. Gardner, what can you tell us about the negotiations? Is it true there might be a deal in the offing?"

"Can you explain what terms are agreed at this stage?"

"When are we likely to see a full schedule resumed?"

"Have you anything to say to the thousands of customers who have been left high-and-dry this week, Ms. Gardner?"

"What do you say to the growing demands for compensation?"

The reporters swarmed around Heather as she stepped from the black Lincoln Town Car at the hotel entrance. But she left their questions hanging unanswered in the damp air. Head down and brandishing the words "No comment" like a verbal shield, she pushed her way through the mass of bodies, cameras and microphones until she eventually made it to the calm of the lobby.

The CEO was the only one doing media.

She checked her coat with the concierge and then hurried towards the conference room; her tap on the elevator call button was far stronger than intended. She needed to calm down. Deep breaths.

Stepping out onto the mezzanine, an assistant crossed quickly to greet her and explained that the Board was still dealing with another matter. Heather took a seat and another intake of breath, glad for a moment to sit quietly and gather her thoughts. But those damn words were still there, gnawing at her.

Heather was SVP, Human Resources at a major airline, a company where the scale of internal conflict had spiraled completely out of control. Four disputes, official and otherwise, within the previous two years was damning evidence that there were serious underlying problems at play.

She had been brought onboard only a number of months previously to help the new CEO transform labor relations across the business. So far, it had been an uphill struggle, to put it mildly, and this most recent high-profile disruption was the subject of intense media coverage because it had brought countrywide operations to a standstill. Thousands were affected by it, directly and indirectly, and there were plenty of angry customers around who were only too happy to vent their fury across the national airwaves.

Apart from these periodic blow-outs that got all the publicity, daily life within the business was a constant struggle for everyone involved; soul-destroying was a term that frequently came to mind. Heather had just been summoned from the strike negotiations by the Board for what she was told would be an opportunity to provide members with an update on current developments, but more importantly, to give them a no-holds-barred assessment of where the root problems lay for the constant disputes. They were clearly sick and tired of the negative publicity and more likely, the damage done to earnings and profitability as a result of the all too frequent stoppages over recent years.

As she waited, Heather knew that nobody blamed her for the current problems; she hadn't been around long enough to have caused, or indeed to have been in a position to fix, them. But she felt under the microscope nonetheless. First of all working alongside the CEO and others, she had to strike the right balance at the negotiations. They needed to get the deal right. A far from easy task.

Added to that her overall analysis of the root problems facing the company – the fresh-pair-of-eyes-perspective – which she had been asked to deliver to the Board had to be credible. It was a big deal for her, a first test at this level, and she needed to project well in the short time available. She most definitely did not want to come across as some pink-and-fluffy chick from HR.

A door opened and she was asked to join the meeting.

Heather stood, quickly glanced at her appearance in the gold-plated mirror by the marble fireplace, fixed her jacket collar slightly and then entered into what could best be described as a tense atmosphere.

The initial questions she faced centered upon the present status of the negotiations.

She explained that there had been progress in line with the terms that the Board had broadly signed-off upon the previous day. All the operational and relationship issues had been addressed, she said, and it was just a matter of the financial implications being agreed; the CFO was currently leading that section of the discussions. It looked as if there would be a draft deal to consider later that evening.

With the current position established the focus quickly shifted to the deeper problems at the airline. The questioning on that front began.

The Chairman opened by asking Heather to tell them a little more about the range of problems she had seen in the business since joining, issues she felt either fuelled, or resulted from the constant conflict.

She decided to begin with a little story that she assured them would place the problems starkly in context.

An hour earlier, during a break in the negotiations, she explained how she had been chatting to a talented, but clearly de-motivated supervisor – a junior member of the union team. To her surprise the guy had suggested several positive things that would make a difference to efficiency in his department and could be applied when they got back to work. When she had asked him why he had not told his manager about these great ideas he had delivered a blunt, but very revealing response: "I don't get paid from the neck up."

Heather paused for a moment to let the words sink in. She felt released; the gnawing stopped.

This, she highlighted, was the attitude of a supervisor and he was far from an outlier either. She went on to explain that when you dropped down another rung on the ladder in the business, the negativity was even more pronounced at times. This had a direct impact on the quality of service offered to customers which in turn contributed to the poor financial performance seen in recent years.

She looked at each of the faces around the table and awaited a reaction.

One of the Board members spoke up. He demanded that the individual in question be fired on the spot. "If he doesn't feel paid from the neck up, then we damn well won't pay him at all," he virtually screamed, as he momentarily lost composure.

For an instant her heart sank because she felt the real point had been completely missed.

Thankfully the Chairman didn't follow that line of argument, but instead asked her to explain how she thought matters had deteriorated to such an extent within the company.

At that point, Heather knew that she needed to get the message across to the Board that, until the conflict was dealt with and engagement levels increased, the company would likely continue to lurch from one crisis to another. Radical change was now required, not simply tinkering around at the edges, papering over the cracks, or attempting to fire all and sundry as had been the norm in the past. She had to get the Board members onside with the rationale for deep-rooted change. This was her big chance. She decided to go for broke.

She responded by explaining that there had been a tendency in the past at the airline to blame the difficulties on intransigent employees, or more specifically, their union representatives. In fact this was precisely what the previous management team had done, which only served to make matters worse. Her assessment of the situation, however, was that some managers, at all levels, were equally, if not more, to blame than the employees for the problems.

Out of the corner of her eye she could see the scowls developing on the faces of one or two in the room. But she kept going.

In her view, she explained, there had been a total collapse of meaningful leadership throughout the airline, which over time had led to – amongst the many other problems – rampant conflict and high levels of employee disengagement. She added that it was also clear to her that, even during past negotiations, there hadn't been any real engagement. Although each and every one of the previous disputes had been 'resolved' all that had happened when everyone went back to work was that both parties sought to create a situation where they could recoup the losses suffered during the negotiations, be they tangible or emotional deficits.

In the case of certain managers this meant turning the screw on employees at every available opportunity which only served to taint the atmosphere even further; for some employees this simply meant making life as difficult as possible for their bosses, or for the more militant workers, sabotaging expensive equipment as a way of venting their anger and frustration.

From what she could see the only outcome arising from the previous conflict resolution negotiations was that they simply had patched over the real problems that lay deep within the business; they merely represented milestones on a downward trajectory. Those mistakes could not be repeated this time.

As she spoke a little voice in her head reminded her that she shouldn't be overly negative either; she didn't want to get tagged as some sort of doom-and-gloom merchant – 'Happy Heather', or similar, would probably be the sarcastic nickname given to her if she appeared to be indulging in a moan-fest – so she also highlighted that the future was not entirely bleak.

Since the current CEO had been appointed and a largely new senior management team, including her, recruited, she emphasized how they were trying to depersonalize the conflict and reverse the buildup of hostilities that had occurred over many years. Clearly they hadn't, as yet, succeeded in that aim but there were some encouraging signs that the level of animosity was declining. She was confident that, when this dispute was over, they could make strong inroads into addressing the underlying issues and rebuilding relationships that would ultimately increase engagement levels.

After a brief silence the Chairman thanked Heather for her honesty. Although there was little sentiment in his tone the words alone helped to calm her nerves. Still she could tell by the faces of some in the room that her bluntness was not entirely welcome. She had a strange feeling that one or two were happy to give her just enough rope to see what she might do with it.

Another Board member spoke up and asked her to offer more insights into where the problems lay.

Heather decided to give another practical example to make her point. She began to describe a recent meeting she had held with a team of managers in the baggage-handling section of the airline. During those discussions, she explained, the terms 'them' and 'us' almost exclusively were used by those present to distinguish members of management from ordinary employees. This type of thinking, she added, was rife throughout the company and had clearly built up over many years, resulting in a situation where managers and employees essentially were working from competing sets of goals, as opposed to focusing on a shared future. The culture was one of confrontation and, although it was an outcome of what had happened in the past, it also fuelled further conflict, so she felt that it was almost like a vicious circle in some respects.

At that point the Board member interrupted and asked her to be more specific about how the cultural problems showed themselves every day.

Where to start in answering that question was Heather's first thought. She decided to highlight another big issue – that of 'conditioning' – which she felt was a reflection of the cultural problems and was also both an outcome and a driver of the conflict. She explained how the company had suffered greatly because managers and employees had become conditioned to responding in a fairly predictable manner to triggers from the 'other side' – another term she said was widely used that further emphasized the cultural divide. Often during heated arguments between the parties, when questioned, the individuals concerned didn't really know why they were fighting, other than giving 'they-started-it' type responses; playground stuff, for sure, but reality of life on the ground where there had been a total cultural meltdown.

Worse still she felt that a really concerning part of this conditioning was how there was almost a resignation that the problems at the airline would never be resolved. "This is just how it works around here," she explained, was a phrase heard repeatedly since joining the firm.

"You are not trying to tell us that there hasn't been anyone on the operational side who wanted to improve things before now," said one of the scowlers as he began to hitch up the rope.

Growing in confidence Heather quickly countered that she was certainly not saying that no efforts had been made to address the difficulties. The problem, she explained, was not that there weren't people who wanted to break out of the cycle; the issue was that there were not enough of them to make a real difference, to create a tipping point, and more importantly, they weren't supported from the top.

This was, she felt, another striking lesson to be learned from what had happened in the company and it related to just how strong an impact peer pressure can have on the behavior seen in adults.

She continued to explain the point.

"Even though there were managers, and also employees, who did want to find better ways of working together they were often prevented from doing so in the past by others around them, as in one telling example I witnessed where what I would describe as a fairly progressive young manager suffered a verbal assault from his boss, because he was 'wasting time' trying to solicit ideas from his team members on a particular task. He was told in no uncertain terms, 'just tell them what to do' ... It takes a lot of guts to go it alone in those circumstances, so it is often easier to just stay part of the crowd."

"What other problems have you identified?" asked one of the Board members who had been quiet until that point.

"Another important issue is the damage that has been done to overall levels of trust across the airline and again this fuels further difficulties. Clearly the combination of points I have mentioned, and other factors, have resulted in a situation where nobody really trusts one another. Even when there are periods of relative calm in the business both parties seem to spend their time eyeing each other with suspicion, wondering what the other is up to. 'It's too quiet around here, something's stirring', said one manager to me a couple of months ago.

"Everyone likes to talk about lack of communication being one of the core problems," she continued, "but actually it isn't – the real issue is not the quantity of communication but its quality. Seeking open communication has been pointless in the past because neither party accepts what the other is saying as being the truth. So even if they had communicated more, it would have made little difference."

At this the Chairman spoke again and asked Heather what she felt lay at the heart of all the issues identified. By the tone of his questioning this time Heather felt she had gained his support; there would be no lynching today.

She responded to his question by returning to the leadership issue.

At the core of all the problems, she explained, was the lack of leadership that she had touched upon at the beginning, both amongst the management team and indeed from the union representatives. She went on to highlight that, until recently, most of the managers in the company had worked their way up through the ranks – which was good in the sense that they showed loyalty to the airline – but extremely bad for the business because they had learned very limited, and more importantly, very aggressive management styles.

In other words they had never been exposed to alternative approaches to getting the best from people, so it was the case that when the hammer didn't work, they only knew how to reach for a bigger hammer; not only had the main philosophy of leadership been one of a top-down approach, but the styles applied by many managers in the past were somewhere to the right of Attila the Hun. She explained that, similarly, shop stewards and other more senior union representatives had generally worked in this or related industries, so their approach to leading their members also was very blinkered. She recounted a quote from one union leader who had said to her, "If you don't fight for what you want in this place, you get walked on."

"Need I say more," she concluded, without recognizing that she was in danger of lapsing into over-confidence.

A t that point the CEO cut in to capture the points raised so far – and possibly to save Heather from herself – but based on what she knew of him, it was also a signal that he wanted to shift the focus from the past to the future. He asked her what proposals she recommended for moving forward.

She explained that it was clearly going to take some time before they could address substantially the core issues at the company. The pressing concern obviously was to get past the current difficulty and she reminded them that there was some progress to report on that front.

She added that, since the restructuring of the management team and with the new people coming on board, there had been a change in relationships between management and employees – clearly not enough to have prevented this dispute – but enough to mean that, in her view, the levels of intransigence and aggression between the parties was less than had been the case before. She was confident they could build on that foundation.

In the medium term, she stressed, a paradigm shift was needed in terms of how managers and employees interacted right across the company. Of course a clear business strategy was required to return the airline to profitability, but a key component underpinning those plans would be to find ways to fix issues that had led to problems in the past, such as the quality of leadership, effectiveness of communication and employee engagement.

She wrapped up by saying that they had already begun to shift the leadership model at a senior level away from an adversarial approach to one that was partnership-focused. This work, she stressed, had to be continued but the nature of how people were managed within the business had to change at all levels too. If they didn't get the leadership issue right in future, then all other efforts to change the culture and better engage the employees would be wasted.

The CEO highlighted the positives in what she had said but he wanted to see the detail – and any associated costs – before he was willing to sign up for anything. He asked for a full proposal on how the business could move forward and he wanted it within two weeks.

Heather assured him that she would have a detailed set of recommendations ready by then, knowing full well that she was going to be under severe pressure to pull everything together within such a tight timeframe. But her immediate concern was to get back to the negotiations to help get them across the line.

She took her leave of the Board, pleased that she had come across in a positive light.

Later that night she sat with the negotiating team – by then including the CEO – and they put the final touches to the agreement that had been sanctioned by the Board. From that it was a matter of awaiting the union vote which was never certain because they had not got everything they had wanted ...

So that's how it all ended up and 24 hours later, the vote came in and the deal was done. We could all get back to work. Or should I say, then the real work started for me and I have spent the past few days trying to pull together a medium-term framework to change the culture within the business which will help to reduce conflict and increase employee engagement levels," said Heather to her classmates on the CNYU Program.

Nobody quite remembers how they had drifted onto discussing the problems in Heather's company but as they all later agreed, it had been one of the more interesting classes since the program commenced. Gathered as per usual for the second session of the week on Thursday evening, the topic was supposed to have been about employee engagement, and although they had not strayed too far off that general area, they had just spent the past hour listening intently to Heather as she explained what she had been through over the last few weeks.

Now that she was finished Professor Henry stood up and addressed the group. Thanking Heather for her insights he began to sum up the evening.

"It never ceases to amaze me how some managers – and not just in Heather's organization by the way – fail to see the blindingly obvious; how mismanaged conflict can completely destroy business performance. This is something well understood, proven beyond debate, yet some managers either fail to grasp the point, or intentionally choose to ignore it.

"You do not need to be any sort of management expert," he continued, "to figure out that people like to work in positive, uplifting environments and when they find that, they tend to give more in return, to fully engage; or, at least the majority will do so, and in the world of work you can only ever hope to legislate for the majority.

"Employee productivity and motivation are always significantly higher in an environment where levels of conflict are low, than when they are not.

"As I say, none of this is groundbreaking stuff," added the Professor, "the evidence has been heard and the judgment came in a long time ago. So overwhelming, in fact, is the proof confirming the benefits that come from minimizing conflict at work that you would be forgiven for thinking that conflict resolution would be at the top of the agenda for most managers.

"Unfortunately, as we just heard this evening, reality tells us otherwise: indeed, everyone in this room undoubtedly has at least one story to tell about a conflict situation that was left to fester and ultimately led to severe but avoidable problems.

"Apart from this wealth of anecdotal evidence there is also plenty of respected international research that shows unresolved conflict has a negative influence on the levels of engagement seen in many businesses.

"Conflict is, however, a normal human state," he explained, "so the surprise is not that it exists in the workplace, but rather how it is often so badly handled. And it is important to make a distinction here.

"Constructive conflict, which leads to new ideas and better solutions, should be encouraged, but well managed, so that employees feel that they can speak their minds or contribute in an appropriate manner. Destructive conflict, on the other hand, which adds no value, should be dealt with promptly, as a failure to do so impacts on relationships and creates a poisoned atmosphere that ultimately affects business performance.

"Thankfully, most businesses today do not suffer from the extremes that Heather is facing at present, but there are lessons for all of us in what we have heard tonight, which are undoubtedly obvious, but frequently get lost in the mix.

"The first and most critical message is that real leadership – effectively applied at all levels – reduces conflict levels and raises employee engagement. Overall culture too has a direct impact on the nature and quality of relationships within a business and, where conflict is seen as the norm, the majority of employees will disengage. Equally when negative behaviors, be they amongst managers or employees, are tolerated for long periods, people become conditioned to act and behave in a similar fashion. Breaking down any such conditioning therefore must be viewed as a key element in helping to prevent, or move away, from a conflict situation.

"Finally the stronger characters within a business – the informal leaders, if you like – can greatly influence the way others think and behave, so it is important to make sure that they exert a positive influence when seeking to resolve conflict in the workplace.

"As a take away from this session consider the core factors we discussed around conflict and employee engagement to see how they apply to your business. Ask yourself, do they positively contribute to overall performance?

"Thank you. You will have Professor de Vreys again next week."

Change is the law of life. And those who look only to the past or present are certain to miss the future.

John F. Kennedy

SECOND CHANCE

Jay Waldron sped down the on-ramp to join the New England Thruway, only narrowly avoiding clipping the rear of the slow-moving car on the inside lane. When he overtook the idiot, he watched as the 'bird' appeared in his rear-view mirror. He flipped one back. The miles behind him since he had left the city were but a blur. He was still in a state of complete shock.

Once the Professor had asked to see him after class, he had expected some form of dressing-down, a smack on the wrist maybe, for his frequent smart comments and general blasé approach to the program, but no more than that. He was, after all, a paying customer. To be told he was no longer welcome had left him stunned.

As he sat there in the oak-paneled study it had taken some time before the words had fully registered. A man of his age being removed from the course was quite an indictment on where his life stood. Strangely, it was not really the fact that he had been told he was wasting his time and money that got to him most. No, it was more a case that his disinterest had been so transparent.

He was clearly on a slippery slope, one that was apparent to all.

After his father had died the previous year Jay had taken control of the family firm, Waldron Office Furniture, a well-established but fading enterprise that nonetheless employed over 50 people out in Westchester County. The business, a manufacturer of bespoke office furnishings and storage equipment, was established 40 years earlier and at one time, had been a major player in the sector. But with the growth of cheap foreign imports and, truth be known, due to a lack of direction for the business it had been in slow and steady decline for the past decade or more. It was now just about breaking even annually.

Since taking over Jay had applied the same degree of passion and enthusiasm to running the firm as he did to most things in his life: slim to none at all.

He had registered to attend the Executive Development Program at the City of New York University in the hope that exposure to successful managers and entrepreneurs of his own age might instill some sense of drive in him. Deep down he knew that the time had long since passed where he needed to start taking life more seriously and in truth, to start paying his way. Still single and in his mid-30s he had achieved little so far. This was not due to any lack of talent on his behalf, but was more a case that he hadn't found his passion in life. Well, that's what he told himself anyway.

Once more he realized, as he took the exit ramp towards the Boston Post Road, he had been deluding himself, running from reality and expecting that his path in life would magically appear, or that someone else would find the answer for him. He now had no choice but to face facts; the writing on the wall couldn't have been clearer if someone had painted it in giant fluorescent-pink lettering. He was a loser.

If there was to be a purpose in his life, it would not be found through others. It was up to him. Only he could haul himself up the slope.

The weeks after he was bounced from the program were a period of personal crisis for Jay. During that time he wasn't able to concentrate on the business and more or less left it in remote-control-mode, although he knew the Operations Manager would hold the fort capably.

He spent the time trying, as he was reminded from one of the sessions on the course, to figure out what his calling was in life. Yet just as it had done in the classroom setting, it seemed a pointless exercise. The more he focused on where his life was at, and indeed where it was headed, the further he seemed to get from any answers. It all looked pretty bleak.

Then about two months later, during a visit to the cemetery of all places, he had a revelation of sorts.

As he sat by his father's graveside, on the small bench funded and fitted by his loyal employees, Jay reflected on how his dad had built the business from scratch. He thought about the many sacrifices he had made to grow and sustain the company and how his father had been so proud when he, the only son, had decided to return from abroad to join the firm; the Prodigal Son, he sneered to himself, and in a way he was glad that his dad wasn't around to see the mess he was making of his life. And the business.

But Jay knew then as he sat in silence that he had no interest in office furniture. He was faced with what was, in reality, a simple choice – could he create a vision for the business that would energize him, or should he just sell it off to the highest bidder? Take whatever money could be generated and run.

Whilst he weighed the options faced it was then that one of his father's old pals dropped by for a quick chat with his now absent friend, as he apparently did every day. Not wanting to disturb a son's time with his father the little man had turned quietly to leave but Jay, catching him out of the corner of his eye, signaled for him to stay and sit with him for a while.

Resting side by side on the bench, the old man spoke movingly of his departed friend and how much he missed him, regaling Jay with stories from their youth, reminiscences about a life shared between two men who had been friends since childhood. It was when they were discussing how his father had set up the business that the old friend dropped a bombshell.

"You know, Jay, the funny thing is that your father absolutely hated office furniture," he said laughing. "Couldn't stand the stuff."

"Wha …? But he spent most of his life making and selling it, why did he do that if he hated it so much?"

"You see," said the old man, "it wasn't the product that interested your dad, it was the challenge of building something that drove him. It just happened that he spotted a gap in the market for office furniture at the time, could have been anything really. But he was driven, almost obsessively, by the act of creation and in the process the desire to support his own family and, it has to be said, to provide security to his employees so that they could raise theirs.

He loved the business, the people working in it, his customers, but not necessarily the product itself."

For several weeks after that chance encounter those words bothered Jay. He began to feel a change in himself. No, he did not have, nor would he ever develop, any real passion for office furniture but the thoughts of saving and then transforming the business began to play on his mind; that and the challenge of keeping alive what his father had worked so hard to build.

Slowly a new sense of energy and enthusiasm began to grow inside, one that he had never felt before. He spent time examining all elements of the business: researching the market, identifying new trends, examining the books and looking at alternative production processes until, finally, he felt he had a new vision for the company and a broad plan of how he wanted to make that a reality.

It was therefore with great excitement that, about a month after that pivotal meeting in the graveyard, he stood in the cafeteria before the assembled managers and employees and spent 30 minutes outlining his ideas, for once with a true sense of passion.

But instead of being hailed a hero, as he had expected would happen, he was met with a stony silence. When he finished the resentment in the room was palpable. The first comment from the floor was negative, so too was the next. As was the one after that. In fact the general air of negativity grew with every contribution made.

Abruptly he called the meeting to a close and stormed out.

In the weeks following the botched announcement, as he tried to progress his plans, he was met with nothing but resistance on all fronts. Where previously there had rarely been any serious disagreements or conflict he spent his days locking horns with senior managers and key employees at the firm. Incensed that they should turn on him like that Jay was determined, regardless of their unwillingness to accept the new way forward, that he would make the changes happen.

It became a battle of wills, one he was determined not to lose.

The pressure mounted and, following a blazing row, he eventually fired the Operations Manager, a man who had been with the firm for almost 20 years. The night of the sacking, as he tossed and turned in bed, the stress was unbearable for Jay; as was his anger. If they wouldn't change then he would just sell the business and to hell with them all, he thought, as his head pounded and mind raced.

Yet he couldn't just cut and run at the first signs of trouble like he had done all his life. No, he knew he had to stick with this, regardless of how fruitless it all seemed. But he clearly needed help. Then somewhere in the depths of the night, he had an unusual idea.

Jay had been worried that the man might not even take his call. But to his credit, he had greeted him warmly, and not only that, had agreed to give him a hearing. Jay then proceeded to describe for him what had happened within the business over the previous months – his new sense of purpose for the firm – but also the floundering attempts to achieve a radical change in direction. In short, he explained to the man at the other end of the line, he needed help and wondered whether, for an appropriate fee of course, he might be willing to visit the business and advise him as to how he might proceed.

Expecting a negative response he was both surprised and delighted when the offer was accepted; the fact that he also had been told that a fee would not be required said something about the caliber of the person he was dealing with.

Some days later Professor de Vreys spent a full day touring the operation, talking with key managers and employees, speaking on the phone to customers and consulting with colleagues who knew more about the industry sector than he did. He quickly had gained a strong understanding of the business and, in particular, what had gone wrong with regard to the change process.

He felt that, to his credit, Jay had identified a viable vision for the company. Jay also had developed a broad roadmap for how to get there, involving a radical overhaul of all aspects of the operation: from the range of products to be offered, with regard to the markets to be targeted and including the major proposal to retain the design function but to outsource the manufacturing process, thereby reducing the overall cost base. In essence the firm would shift from a focus on manufacturing to one of design and client servicing.

However it was pretty clear too that Jay had made some fundamental mistakes when it came to managing the change process itself. As they sat over a coffee in the late afternoon the Professor flagged some important issues.

"Jay, when your dad was alive, what sort of relationship did he have with his employees?"

"He was very dedicated to them, sort of like a father figure to each and every one. He felt that they were almost like an extended family and he wanted to look after them as best he could. That was part of the problem because he didn't make the necessary changes and, as a consequence, the business lost its edge."

"Undoubtedly there are issues in that regard which we will get to in a moment, but how do you think your father would view the manner in which you have handled the change process so far?"

"Well he likely would have frowned on my approach, but that's hardly surprising."

"That may be the case, Jay, although by seeking to ram through the changes, have you got what you wanted?"

"No, not yet perhaps, but I am dealing with an intransigent bunch of people who have had it far too easy for far too long."

"My own view, having spoken to the key managers and employees at length today, is that, even though they are long-serving, they also seem to understand that radical change is required. In fact, many of them have said to me that it was your dad who did not want to change in the past, not the other way around.

"So given the profile of your people, I think – actually I know – that not consulting with them about your vision and presenting it as a *fait accompli* was a big mistake. Not only did you ignore their loyalty and dedication to the business but you potentially missed out on the many good ideas they have for helping take the company in a new direction."

"Sorry, Professor, I disagree. Clearly with my proposals there are going to be job losses on the manufacturing side of things, so it's a bit like asking turkeys to vote for Thanksgiving – they are hardly going to work with me to put themselves out of a job."

"Actually this is a good example of what happens when communication around change is lacking – you get serious misconceptions on both sides. First of all you should really give your people more credit. They are well aware that the manufacturing element is uncompetitive and that the future for the business therefore lies in design, installation and support services. They see that.

"Understandably some of the older generation are concerned that they will not be left completely high and dry in terms of what package, if any, you might consider to 'put them out to graze', as they described it. Others are prepared to retrain into different aspects of the business. Everyone said they would take pay-cuts if that meant more jobs could be saved.

"In short the message is that they will gladly work with you but you have made no attempt to consult or involve them in decision-making. When you do that, you back people into a corner and you get resistance. It is not that hard to figure out.

"In my experience of helping companies cope with change," the professor continued, "and that is not an insignificant number by the way, people struggle with it to varying degrees. Generally speaking the bigger the change, the greater the likelihood they will struggle. Consequently and particularly so when you have a long-serving and loyal team like you do here, you need to get them onboard with the change; if you fail to do that, their natural response is to fear and resist the proposals and they band together to work against you.

"This is precisely what you have created here and you have made the same mistake that many managers do: you assume that as people are likely to resist change in any case, there is no point in consultation.

"Now I am well aware that not every business has the type of employees that you have but consultation always must be a feature of change, even if, in the end, you cannot get their support and have to impose things, it is still vital to begin with a consultative approach. It constantly surprises me that so many managers ignore this and then end up with an unnecessary dispute or even a strike on their hands. And ultimately how are all disputes resolved? Yes, through consultation. Better to start with it, I find."

"So where do I go from here?" asked Jay, feeling like he had just got a scolding.

"Well, from what I have seen, you have a very clear vision of where you want to take the business, so that is a really strong place to be starting from. I have not looked at the numbers in any great detail, but broadly what you are proposing seems to make sense. Now I think you need to step back and begin all over again."

"And what would that entail?"

"Initially I think you should consider reinstating your Operations Manager, if he is still available, because I get the sense that you made that particular decision on emotional, not rational, grounds. I do not know the person in question but the people here certainly hold him in high esteem and this might be important in helping you with the transformation you are proposing."

"But he was resisting my proposals. How can I have someone on board who doesn't share my vision of the future? In any case, he has presided over the *status quo* for too long; if he was that good, he would have come up with his own ideas for improving the performance of the business."

"As I said, Jay, it is a matter for you. I have not met the man but I can tell a little about him from what others have said today. And I would imagine – if you sat and discussed the issue with him – that he, like many others, was not against your proposals *per se* but rather the manner in which you tried to introduce them. Maybe you are right, he might not be a visionary, but that is no bad thing either because what you need is someone who can execute your plans effectively, and he seems more than capable of doing that. In fact from what I gather, he kept the place running well whilst your mind was elsewhere, did he not?

"Remember having the vision for change is important, vital even, but so too is making things happen on the ground so that the vision is realized. That is where many businesses fall down in my experience: good ideas, lousy execution. Think about it, Jay, can you execute as effectively as he can? Ultimately it is your decision."

"And what else do you think I need to do?" asked Jay, shifting a little uncomfortably in his seat as the truth hit home.

"I suggest that you get everyone together again and give them an overview of the big picture: where the business is now, what the really fundamental issues are, why you need to change and, finally, why you believe what you are proposing is the right way forward. Naturally, as part of this, you need to highlight how the changes will impact on people – no point pretending there are no downsides for them – but also to explain that you are prepared to work with them and take their viable ideas on board, in order to minimize the negative impact of the changes that are necessary. In essence you need to help reduce their fears and respond to their concerns."

"What then?"

"Strange as it may sound, Jay, if you get that bit right, the rest will become much easier to manage. If people, or at least the majority, are convinced of the need for change, then the execution process is easier. Of course for that you will still need a clear plan, with roles and responsibilities assigned and deadlines set for progression.

"As part of that, make sure you get, and keep, people actively involved in the planning and implementation process; have them on teams making suggestions on the way forward, or gather their ideas in other ways. But do not let them become bystanders in the change process – bystanders have too much time to dwell on things, worry and indeed find problems.

"And whatever route you do take, make sure not to let the change process run on indefinitely. This is a major transformation of the business you are talking about here so clearly it will not happen overnight, but you still need to define when you will be through to the other side, with milestones on the way defined. There is nothing, and I mean nothing, that will frustrate people more than open-ended change or a process that drags on forever. Get the pain out of the way as quickly as is feasible.

"Then when you start seeing results, even little changes, you should make sure you acknowledge and reward people where appropriate. This will keep them motivated."

"It all sounds so easy, Professor, when you describe it."

"Look, you know that such a radical redesign of your business model is not going to be easy, but the simple fact remains that change is a feature of life in all businesses today, and managers like yourself are constantly faced with handling small and large changes at work. Consequently you personally must be comfortable in dealing with change and in helping your employees to cope with it, particularly those changes that are substantial in nature.

"For major change like you are proposing it is essential that you follow a structured, but not rigid, approach to implementation, one which, as I said, takes into account the not inconsequential people-related issues associated with any change.

"Alright so you got off to a bad start, but from what I can tell from my visit today, all is far from lost. Follow the route we just discussed and I think you will find that the path ahead will be smoother than what you might otherwise imagine."

"Thank you, Professor, not only for coming down to advise me today but for giving me a second chance."

"You are most welcome, Jay. Normally I would not have much time for someone I had asked to leave one of my programs, but the look of devastation on your face when I spoke to you that evening told me that you cared. You clearly did not know at that time what you cared about but I knew you had the capacity to find something that mattered to you. Now that you have found it I am happy to support you. May I wish you every success with your proposals."

The only thing we know about the future is that it will be different.

Peter Drucker

NEW BEGINNINGS

Heather and Jane stood huddled together under the heat lamp outside the neighborhood deli on Trinity Place, enjoying their coffee in the dim November sunshine. They were sharing gossip and a cigarette as they waited for the guys to arrive.

"Gotta give these things up in the New Year," said Jane, as she screwed her face at the lingering taste of smoke.

"Yeah, it's enough already," replied Heather. "No wonder we're still single, no man will come near us because we smell like ashtrays."

They laughed but knew that, in this city, she was not a million miles from the truth.

Changing the subject rapidly they talked about the year gone by, how much they had gained from it, and both expressed similar feelings of sadness that the program was coming to an end.

"Although I won't miss the workload, that's for sure," said Jane, as she pretended to pull her hair out.

"Hey ladies."

The shout came from down the block, followed by a sad attempt at a wolf-whistle. It was Karl, a broad grin on his face, closely followed by Mike who, as usual, had his cell phone stuck to his ear. They all greeted each other as the good friends they had become since being assigned together as a team for the second half of the course; the slight lingering look between Jane and Mike did not go unnoticed by Heather.

Having grabbed some more coffees to go, they walked the few blocks to collect Karl's car before setting off on their two-hour journey.

J ack Rosner looked out through the large bay window. "This is my kingdom," he said to himself, laughing at the absurdity of the thought. He was standing in his favorite meeting room, staring vacantly down onto the gardens below and sort of daydreaming as he waited for the group to arrive. From its bright yellows to the vibrant reds, the late Fall foliage was as breathtaking as ever; on days like this he never ceased to wonder at Nature's splendor. He loved this place. And what it stood for.

A light tap at the door brought him round.

A young waiter entered and placed a tray of sandwiches on the sideboard. He lit the lamp under the soup tureen and, having checked with Jack that all was in order, he then quietly left.

Jack stepped away from the window and took a seat at the baize-covered table. He poured himself a glass of water and began to scan through his notes from the previous meeting. And as he refreshed his memory on earlier discussions, he thought about his achievements.

Twenty years before he had bought a rundown hotel in Connecticut and he was now the proud owner of 10 small resort hotels across the Northeast. To cap it all, six months earlier, his little hotel group had achieved the American Hotel Association Business Excellence Award, the only company on the East coast to do so. It was a big deal. The recognition of peers always was.

And it was all the more satisfying because it hadn't just happened by chance.

Many years back Jack had made a conscious effort to harness the input of his management team and employees in the running of the business and to provide a clear structure for everything they did. He was keen for them to become true partners and in particular, he wanted to involve his senior managers more closely in driving the future development of the hotels.

Of course he expected them to continue giving their all towards managing day-to-day operations but he also wanted them to start looking further out onto the horizon, to be more focused on the future so that they could make a real contribution, both to the definition and achievement of longer-term goals.

The approach had worked because not only had profitability grown in a pretty shaky market but the award signified that they were now considered to be leaders in their field. He was a proud man.

Reviewing the agenda he had been sent for the afternoon's meeting Jack was reminded too how he had been more than a little surprised the previous September when the call had come through from a Professor de Vreys at CNYU. He had asked Jack whether he would be willing to participate in a project the University was organizing for mid-career executives attending one of its development programs.

The Professor had explained that, as an award-winning enterprise, his hotel company was an ideal location to take program participants completely out of their comfort zone so that – as the objective of the project specified – they could pinpoint what drove business success, in any field. Given that none of the four members of the team he was proposing to allocate to Jack's business had any background in the hospitality industry, he felt that his company was a perfect choice.

In truth, Jack had been flattered by the attention and was honored to participate; he was not above having his ego massaged occasionally. And that is how he ended up sitting in the conference room at his flagship hotel in Lakeville awaiting the arrival of the four executives.

They already had made one visit to another of his properties a month earlier and this second visit, they had explained in the covering note accompanying the agenda, was designed to bridge any knowledge gaps so that they could finalize their project.

The phone by his side rang. "Send them straight up," he said.

When they arrived in the room a light lunch was shared and then they got down to work. Mike opened the discussions.

"Jack, thanks again for taking the time out to see us. Our first meeting was a great help and we now have a pretty good understanding of where your company has come from and what your goals are. Today we would like to get a better feel for what you think have been the main factors behind your success, those really key drivers that you believe have guided your achievements and would also be applicable for managers in any business setting."

Jack smiled. If they didn't know already that he liked to talk about his company, then they were about to find out.

"You guys are plenty experienced so you already know that it's really a combination of many diverse factors that drives success; 'there ain't no easy answers' as I always say. That said, many years ago I developed a simple management model for us to follow in the business, one that was fairly substantial in nature, integrated all important activities but at the same time was user-friendly and easy to communicate.

"Now I don't pretend there is anything magic about this four-part model but I do believe that it brings together all elements that are essential to achieving success, in any business. It forms the basis for everything we do here. And given what we have achieved to date, the model must be doing something right for us."

He handed each of them a single sheet of paper upon which the four-part framework was drawn. He then continued.

"The first part of the model is essentially about direction, or in other words, it's concerned with defining where the hell we are going. I'm a big believer that success for any business begins with getting a real handle on the future. So a number of years ago, I sat down with my top guys and we developed our vision and mission statements; actually we don't call them that, because those terms sound a bit formal and stuffy to us, but that's essentially what we have.

"As I told my people at the time we needed to define why we were killing ourselves day-in-day-out, what were we trying to achieve? We were doing this for a reason, so I wanted to capture those motivations. And that's what we did.

"Every company, regardless of size, needs what I like to call a strategic umbrella to guide decision-making – a framework under which everything fits. And that context begins with figuring out where the business is headed, but also by deciding what it is all about as an entity. I really emphasized back then that I didn't believe that our 'purpose' was solely to make a profit ..."

He paused for a moment and smiled at the group.

"Now let me be very clear before you shift me off to a nursing home, profit is essential but I wanted my people to understand that it is the desired outcome from, and not necessarily the sole reason for, running our business."

Jack stopped briefly again to let those particular words sink in. He felt this was a critical point to highlight. He truly believed that to rise above the norm, to deliver sustained advantage, there must be a driving force behind a business beyond the profit motive.

He expanded on this train of thought.

"To tell you the truth if it was only about pure profit for me, then I'd probably close the hotels and invest the money elsewhere; the returns in other sectors are much better and I could be off sunning myself on a yacht in the Caribbean or something. But I love this industry, it's an addiction to be honest, and of course I want to make money – yet I want to do so in a way that provides lasting value for investors, creates memorable experiences for my customers, delivers job security for my employees and makes a positive impact on the local community where the hotels are located.

"It was those sentiments that we captured in our vision and mission statements and they have guided the development of the business for many years."

At this Karl raised a concern about how tools like vision and mission get a lot of bad press because they are widely misused in many organizations. He wondered how Jack had made them work for him.

"You're dead right about that, Karl, and I have seen many times how those statements end up as flowery but meaningless statements in certain companies, pinned to a wall somewhere, slowly fading and curling at the edges, a monument to lost hopes and dreams. Not here.

"As I touched upon a moment ago, the first thing we did was to change the terminology: we have one statement which we call 'Our-Way' and this captures our vision and mission. It has provided a meaningful route map – known to all – from which the business strategy was then developed. Our employees, at all levels, are really focused on Our-Way and I cannot emphasize enough just how much it means to us and how we now look at the business very differently as a result.

"But it doesn't stop there. Making these nice fluffy statements work for you requires a lot more than a simple change in wording.

"To make Our-Way meaningful to the business on a day-to-day basis we translate the broad sentiments contained within it into clear strategic goals which include targets in relation to *Management Goals* – financial targets, and other non-financial goals, for example, in relation to quality, environmental management, hygiene and safety; *Customer Goals* – targets in relation to customer satisfaction, loyalty, retention, market share etc; and *Employee Goals* – goals in relation to employee engagement, turnover, productivity etc. When the goals are set, we then plan how to achieve them."

Jack continued to highlight how he was big on the managing-by-goals concept and that he felt it was still underused in many industries, or sometimes misused. Where goals were developed and applied effectively he had seen how they made a real difference to business performance – they translated broad aspirations into something more concrete and measurable.

He explained that becoming more goal-orientated had served as a real focus for his senior management team and, more importantly, the strategies and plans developed to realize those holistic goals meant that they were moving forward collectively in a clear and organized manner. They all got a great sense of pride, a genuine buzz, as well as financial rewards, when they moved in the right direction towards their targets.

"So that's what the first part of my model is all about, guys – the future, beyond the here and now – because short-termism, for me, is what kills many businesses. Having clear direction, but at the same time making that truly meaningful in terms of actually supporting business development, is a key success driver."

"And could you also tell us a little about the second element of your business model?" asked Jane, pointing to the framework on the sheet in front of her.

"As you can see the next part of the model is all about Effective Leadership – to engage our employees, who will then be motivated to really wow our customers, which in turn makes the money that keeps our investors happy. For me nothing can be achieved in any business without strong leadership, and in its absence, goals and plans – no matter how well defined – will remain but empty wishes.

"Although as you are undoubtedly well aware, there is plenty of nonsense surrounding the topic of leadership, I'm a sort of a spade-is-a-spade guy when it comes to the subject. I want all 'leaders' in my business to be what I describe as *manaleaders*: people who can both manage and lead. I want them to engage fully with their teams, or to lead them, but I also want them to achieve outstanding results, or in other words, to manage their given area of responsibility effectively to realize the relevant goals and targets.

"My belief is that, as the owner, I must set the broad context for leadership in the company – leading by example, if you like – so that those around me understand how they are expected to act and behave. But my guys must step up to the plate in this regard by first seeing themselves as, and then acting like, real leaders. Through building their capabilities, with my support of course, they must work hard to get the best out of their teams.

"Effective leadership or management – call it what you will – to me at least, is not what happens when I am on-site, but how well each hotel performs when I am not there. In that regard I am happy to say that I have good leaders and managers around me."

There was a quiet moment when he said that, as the group seemed to reflect on his comments. They could see the passion flickering in Jack's eyes as he spoke.

"And if you get the manage-lead mix right," he continued, "then you will go a long way towards engaging your employees and if you do that, they will go out of their way to look after your customers. It's not that hard to understand this trickle-down approach but it's a hell of a job to get it happening in practice.

"I once heard Sir Richard Branson speak at a travel conference and he mentioned something on this issue that really stuck with me. He said something to the effect that 'loyal employees in a company create loyal customers, who in turn create happy shareholders. The process sounds easy but it is not, and it has defeated some of the bigger organizations of the 20th century'. I think he hit the nail on the head there.

"And I really do believe that we have done the right things in that regard for a long time now, so the leader-employee-customer-investor link is well embedded in our culture at this stage."

Having explained his general philosophy of leadership Jack went on to describe the third component of his management model which he believed was critical in terms of achieving business success in any context. It related to Execution.

This is an area, he felt, where many companies underperformed. It was all well and good to have a strong strategic context, great leadership and engaged employees but that amounted to little if the execution wasn't right. Things have to happen on the ground, he stressed. He explained how he was a strong believer that, in order to make the business goals a reality, there had to be concrete plans in place. Nobody with a wishy-washy hope-for-the-best mentality survived for long in his company.

In each of his hotels this meant preparing an annual business plan to bring the goals to life. This integrated plan, which was prepared with input from all managers and employees – appropriate to their level of course – combined the financial, marketing, HR and operational measures to be addressed in any given year in order to progress the business towards the goals. It was the annual 'bible' for the business.

Of course, in larger enterprises, he knew that more people would likely be involved in the planning process, or that the process itself might be more sophisticated, but the basic principle that execution must be planned and structured held true in every enterprise.

He also emphasized that another important aspect of execution was ensuring that all key processes in any business were as effective as they could be. This, he made clear to the group, was a vital consideration and it didn't matter whether it was a small hotel or a multinational corporation. Execution happens through a framework of key processes – everything from financial management to marketing to customer relationship management – and all processes in a business need to be enhanced and continuously improved to ensure maximum efficiency and effectiveness, using whatever tools, techniques and models worked best for that business.

Jack closed that part of the discussion with what he believed to be a straightforward but insightful statement.

"We need to continuously plan the operation so that we 'do things right' in terms of customer service and so on. But that is of no value unless we 'do the right things' to achieve our goals. Having an annual plan for each of the hotels and ensuring that all our key processes are as effective as possible drives execution so that the future we want is actually realized."

Once more it was obvious that what Jack said had resonated strongly with the group in front of him. He had quickly grown to like the four people sitting opposite and the discussion flowed easily between them.

They had spent an hour and a half on the first three elements of the model, and as time was rapidly moving on, they agreed to start winding down the discussions.

"Perhaps you might tell us a little about the final part of your model to round things off?" asked Mike.

"The fourth and final part of our management model is the area of Performance Measurement and Review, which is of course vital in any business. We have identified global performance measures – financial and non-financial – for the company overall, as well as those for our individual key processes. With this dashboard of measures to monitor our performance we now have a much broader, and I would say more useful, analysis of how the company is really doing.

"We always stay on top of those measures too and any signs of slippage are met with a clear investigation of cause-and-effect and appropriate action is taken to bring us back on track."

They discussed how many businesses, even their own, had a tendency to focus too narrowly on operational and financial metrics, which did not always tell the true story of performance. Heather gave a good example of how in her company, a leading airline, a focus on increasing load-factors – the passenger carrying capacity – had meant that they had attempted to compete with low-cost competitors whilst carrying a high fixed cost base. They were filling the planes, so that particular number looked good but the extra revenue was not converting into profitability because of the lack of margin.

Worse still, she explained, if they had analyzed customer feedback more closely they would have seen how they were alienating a lot of their corporate travelers who did not always appreciate flying *en masse* with the cheap travel brigade. Sometimes, she highlighted, a focus on too narrow a range of measures meant that problems went unnoticed elsewhere in the business.

After a good examination of similar issues the team agreed that they had everything they needed. All that remained was to add the information gathered from that afternoon's discussions to their almost completed report and then email it to Professor de Vreys before 9pm that evening for the final deadline.

They thanked Jack for his time and he took his leave; he was rushing down to the city to speak at an event later that evening. To their surprise he invited them to have dinner at the hotel and indeed to stay overnight if they wished. They hadn't intended to do so but collectively decided to accept. Kind offers like that didn't come along too often.

After Jack left they tidied up their report, highlighting the fact that although his four-point model for success was simple, it was far from simplistic – a quote that Mike and Jane were adamant they should include. These four areas – Direction, Leadership, Execution and Review – whilst undoubtedly complex, offered a clear template for owners and managers in any business to guide decision-making and forward planning.

The framework, they agreed, brought together into one place all that needed to be done to improve the chances of success, from defining the broad strategic context, to creating goals and strategies, to leading and engaging employees, to execution and finally, to the measurement of progress.

With 15 minutes to spare they saved the final document and forwarded it to the Professor by email. Their program was essentially over. They looked at one another with a sense of finality and a bit of a downer hit as each drifted into private thought.

"Now, let's hit the bar and have dinner," said Mike, breaking the somber mood before it took too deep a hold.

During the meal they reflected on the past months and what each one of them would take from the program.

"For me one key message has really hit home this year: not to over-complicate management. By keeping things simple you have a better chance of success than if you go overboard on models and terminology and whether you think of yourself as a leader or manager is not really the point, because you need to do both," said Jane.

"Unfortunately I can't say that I have found my Why in my career as yet, but I know there is something out there that will eventually show itself to me. I have really enjoyed the course, a fantastic experience." She ended by raising her glass in toast to new-found friends.

Heather again noticed the slightly longer than necessary look, and what appeared to be knowing smiles, between Jane and Mike, but once more decided to say nothing. She would get to the bottom of that little matter later.

"When I look back on the year," said Karl, "I think we covered a lot of ground and the 'hard' topics like corporate finance and economics will really stand to me in developing my business in the years ahead. But on the 'soft' side of things, the need for managers to have a positive mindset and a real passion for what they do is a critical point that will remain with me.

"As you know, I need to stay upbeat, not only for health reasons, but in a work context I want to continue to set the example for my team in terms of how I face up, and respond, to challenges.

"We've had a tough year at my company, financially I mean, but I can sense that things are picking up which hopefully will continue in the year ahead. Upbeat and upwards is my new motto," he said, with slightly more enthusiasm than was called for.

The girls joined in as Mike teased Karl on his little Mr. Motivator moment.

They all laughed too as they shared examples of poor leaders they knew who brought an air of negativity into the building every day and how that not only affected their own performance but that of their employees as well. Karl also made a point about how it was obvious that Jack's passion and enthusiasm for the hospitality business had rubbed off on his people as the hotel was full of employees whom you could tell were really 'into' what they were doing for a living.

"What stood out for me about this year is not really a new lesson at all but one which has certainly been reinforced," said Heather. "I think it is critical for managers to have the ability to be flexible. Anyone who has a rigid style is really very limited as a manager in this day-and-age, worse still if that rigidity is stuck at the aggressive end of the scale.

"The fact that you need to have the ability to maintain self-control in order to be flexible also was not new to me, but just how important that is in practice will stay with me as one of the main learning points from the year. Hopefully I can apply those lessons in the months ahead as we continue to try to turn things around at the airline. There is no shortage of people and situations at present that could wind me up if I let them, so I definitely have to keep my cool."

And then the focus turned to Mike. At first he talked a lot about what he would take away from the program and in particular how he felt that the importance of communication, in terms of leadership effectiveness, was still overlooked.

"I think what will stay with me most," he continued, "is the idea that, for all of us to become the best managers that we can be, we need the right mix between our attitude, attributes and actions to help us succeed. It is as much who we are and how we think that will determine the extent of our future success as it is what we do.

"Also fingers crossed that I have enough of the right stuff to help me get that promotion I was telling you all about, should know within a few days. Here's hoping ... well, guys, it's been ... how do you say ... emotional," he ended, with a smile.

They raised their glasses once more, in wishing Mike the best for the upcoming decision, in wider recognition for all their achievements to date and in prospect of an even brighter future. It had been a tough but worthwhile experience, one that they all hoped would set them up for the next part of their careers.

After dinner as they strolled through the gardens in the chill November air, Jane and Heather walked slightly behind the guys.

"And did you find something else this year that you haven't told us about, Jane?" asked Heather as she gently elbowed her now close friend.

"Whatever do you mean?" came the reply, the broad smile on her face indicating that indeed she had.

He that is good for making excuses is seldom good for anything else.

Benjamin Franklin

THE WOOD FOR THE TREES

Feet propped on the desk, he stared out his office window, looking down on the lunchtime crowd below as they mingled at the farmer's market in Richard Tucker Square.

"The world is full of fools," he mumbled to himself. "Oh, look at the homemade breads. Ah, aren't these eggs so big, not like the ones you buy in the supermarket. OMG, I've never seen such fresh-looking salad," he said in mocking tone. "You bunch of idiots, it's probably all just repackaged crap from Walmart."

Swaying slowing from side to side in his leather chair, and throwing an admiring glance at the perfect shine of his shoes, he twirled his pen with his fingers. He was pretty pissed off; more than that, he had been fit to kill for the past 24 hours or so.

Since the great betrayal was perpetrated, that is.

"Baa, baa, baa," he muttered, as he watched the long queue form at the organic lamb stand.

It was clearly time for him to move on. Obviously there was little point in staying with a company where his talents were not appreciated, or worse still, where promotions were not decided on merit. Everyone knew that he had been the better candidate for the position, but somehow politics had put paid to that hope; some might say, that entitlement. He had delivered everything asked of him by the CEO and those other Judases in the C-suite. But, it had all meant nothing in the end.

Somehow that other fool must have found the inside track because there was no way he got the position on talent alone.

And from what he had heard the previous evening from the guys down at the club that was precisely what must have happened. Apparently the guy's dad was some sort of former big-shot around town – 'Boss Hogg' or some such name they had sneered disparagingly – so he must have called in a favor for his son or something: pulled a few strings, cashed some chips. Yes, that must have been it. Nothing else made sense.

It was hard to take but he had been outplayed in The Game.

As he swiveled in the chair, he thought back to the previous day and specifically to what the CEO had said to him when breaking the news that he hadn't made it onto the Operating Committee. He had spouted all the usual platitudes: it was a close run thing *blah-blah-blah*. What-ever.

The boss had raised other issues too about the need to work on his communication skills, to be less manipulative and more collaborative, but he certainly wasn't going to place too much emphasis on any of that nonsense. After all the CEO did have to make something up to justify why he hadn't been successful. Those criticisms were simply an attempt to defend the indefensible. Anyway, his results in the Division were second to none and the last product launch had been faultless, so what else mattered in terms of getting promoted?

He continued staring out the window and started making moo-moo sounds under his breath. *Organic milk, my ass.*

To hell with them anyway, he thought. There were plenty of places in this city where his talents would be better appreciated. All that was needed was a call to a headhunter and within a few days he would have something else lined up. The past four years would just have to be written-off as an error of judgment; he could not have known that there wouldn't be a fair crack of the whip given, that the deck was going to be stacked in someone else's favor.

No, all he could do was to learn from the experience and move on. It was confirmed, yet again, that talent didn't win out in the end. It was really about who, and not what, you knew. The manner of the OC appointment proved that beyond any doubt.

And the biggest personal lesson in all this?

He had better start working a hell of a lot harder at building his network if he was to succeed on such an uneven playing field.

He swung the chair around to the desk, plunked his feet on the floor and fished out the headhunter's number. She would likely be out to lunch, so he would call her later. In the meantime, he thought, best to start going through the files to see what of value could be taken with him when he left.

Steve Howley was looking to the future.

A FINAL WORD FROM THE AUTHOR

This book was intended first and foremost to be an easy read. I sincerely hope it has been that. Having now reached the end, hopefully you will have pinpointed some of the important messages woven within the text also.

Maybe the stories have helped you to reflect on aspects of who you are, or how you think, that you might like to change or improve in future. You also might have thought about elements of what you do – such as your leadership style, how you communicate, handle conflict or manage change – and perhaps you have identified some scope for improvement in those areas too.

Only you can map out how you want to progress from here.

As you do so, if personal improvement is to be on your agenda, then at all times recognize that a desire to change and the ability to actually follow through on that are two different things entirely. We all make New Year's resolutions but how many do we actually stick with beyond February? Not too many, I wager.

In an article entitled *Change or Die* published in *Fast Company* magazine, and later expanded upon in his book of the same name, Alan Deutschman highlighted a number of startling points about our collective inability to change that you should think about. Here is an extract of his article:

> *... What if a well-informed, trusted authority figure said you had to make difficult and enduring changes in the way you think and act? If you didn't, your time would end soon – a lot sooner than it had to. Could you change when change really mattered? When it mattered most?*
>
> *Yes, you say?*

Try again.

Yes?

You're probably deluding yourself.

You wouldn't change.

Don't believe it? You want odds? Here are the odds, the scientifically studied odds: nine to one. That's nine to one against you. How do you like those odds?

Where do those odds come from? In his article, Deutschman refers to a presentation given by Dr. Edward Miller, the Dean of the Medical School and CEO of the Hospital at Johns Hopkins University, which highlights an individual's inability to change:

... He [Dr Miller] turned the discussion to patients whose heart disease is so severe that they undergo bypass surgery, a traumatic and expensive procedure that can cost more than $100,000 if complications arise. About 600,000 people have bypasses every year in the United States, and 1.3 million heart patients have angioplasties – all at a total cost of around $30 billion. The procedures temporarily relieve chest pains but rarely prevent heart attacks or prolong lives. Around half of the time, the bypass grafts clog up in a few years; the angioplasties, in a few months. The causes of this so-called restenosis are complex. It is sometimes a reaction to the trauma of the surgery itself. But many patients could avoid the return of pain and the need to repeat the surgery – not to mention arrest the course of their disease before it kills them – by switching to healthier lifestyles. Yet very few do.

"If you look at people after coronary-artery bypass grafting two years later, 90% of them have not changed their lifestyle," Miller said. "And that's been studied over and over and over again. And so we're missing some link in there. Even though they know they have a very bad disease and they know they should change their lifestyle, for whatever reason, they cannot."

If change, even when life or death is at stake, is so difficult then it is not that hard to figure out why personal change of any kind is such a challenge.

What you do with any insights arising from this book is of course entirely up to you but standing still should never be the preferred choice.

Is it possible to change or improve your performance? Absolutely, it is.

Is that likely to be easy? Absolutely it is not, even more so if it relates to aspects of the right stuff like increasing self-awareness, changing mindsets or building personal characteristics.

Whatever you decide to do, consider the following question: would you be happy if those around you thought of you as a second-rate manager?

I didn't think so.

Take small steps, take them consistently every day and, over time, they will lead to big changes for the better.

I wish you continued success in leadership.

And in life.

THE AUTHOR

Enda Larkin has held senior management positions in Ireland, UK and the US and has worked as a management development consultant since 1994. He has led diverse consulting projects in the hotel, tourism, aviation and banking sectors throughout Europe and the Middle East. As well as designing and delivering leadership programs, he also coaches top executives to maximize their potential as leaders. He holds a BSc in Management from Trinity College Dublin and an MBA from ESCP Europe in Paris.

He is author of *Ready to Lead?* (Pearson/Prentice Hall, 2007), *How to Run a Great Hotel* (How to Books, 2009), *Quick Win Leadership* (Oak Tree Press, 2010) and is a regular contributor to a variety of online and print journals and magazines. He also has written several fiction short stories that have been listed for literary prizes.

He may be contacted at **enda.larkin@htc-consult.com**. Read and subscribe to his daily blog, *The Manager's Toolkit*, which offers useful management articles at **www.endalarkin.com**.

OAK TREE PRESS

Oak Tree Press develops and delivers information, advice and resources for entrepreneurs and managers. It is Ireland's leading business book publisher, with an unrivalled reputation for quality titles across business, management, HR, law, marketing and enterprise topics. NuBooks is its recently-launched imprint, publishing short, focused ebooks for busy entrepreneurs and managers.

In addition, through its founder and managing director, Brian O'Kane, Oak Tree Press occupies a unique position in start-up and small business support in Ireland through its standard-setting titles, as well training courses, mentoring and advisory services.

Oak Tree Press is comfortable across a range of communication media – print, web and training, focusing always on the effective communication of business information.

Oak Tree Press, 19 Rutland Street, Cork, Ireland.

T: + 353 21 4313855 F: + 353 21 4313496.

E: info@oaktreepress.com W: www.oaktreepress.com.

Lightning Source UK Ltd.
Milton Keynes UK
UKOW052108180412

190988UK00001B/4/P